EXPANSE

First published in Great Britain 2025 by Expanse, a part of Farshore
An imprint of HarperCollins*Publishers*
1 London Bridge Street, London SE1 9GF
www.farshore.co.uk

HarperCollins*Publishers*
Macken House, 39/40 Mayor Street Upper,
Dublin 1, D01 C9W8, Ireland

Written by Hannah Verdier

This book is an original creation by Farshore
© 2025 HarperCollins*Publishers* Limited

This book is 100% independent and unofficial and is not endorsed by and has no connection with the people or persons featured, or with any organisation or individual connected in any way whatsoever with the people or persons featured. Every care has been taken in the researching and writing of this book but due to the nature of the subject matter some information may change over time.

Additional imagery used under license from Shutterstock.com

ISBN 978 0 00 875658 1
Printed in Romania
001

A CIP catalogue record for this title is available from the British Library.

All rights reserved. No part of this publication may be reproduced, stored in a retrieval system, or transmitted in any form or by any means, electronic, mechanical, photocopying, recording or otherwise, without the prior permission of the publisher and copyright owner.

Without limiting the author's and publisher's exclusive rights, any unauthorised use of this publication to train generative artificial intelligence (AI) technologies is expressly prohibited. HarperCollins also exercise their rights under Article 4(3) of the Digital Single Market Directive 2019/790 and expressly reserve this publication from the text and data mining exception.

Stay safe online. Farshore is not responsible for content hosted by third parties.

This book contains FSC™ certified paper and other controlled sources to ensure responsible forest management.
For more information visit: www.harpercollins.co.uk/green

100% UNOFFICIAL

OASIS
ANNUAL 2026

CONTENTS

14

- **8** YOU AND I ARE GONNA LIVE FOREVER
- **10** ROCK 'N' ROLL STARS
- **12** OASIS TIMELINE: 1991 – 2000
- **14** OASIS TIMELINE: 2000 – 2025
- **16** LITTLE BY LITTLE
- **18** THE EARLY DAYS
- **20** ALBUM SPOTLIGHT: *DEFINITELY MAYBE*
- **22** COOL BRITANNIA
- **24** OASIS: OFF THE CHARTS!
- **26** DON'T LOOK BACK IN ANGER
- **27** WIBBLING RIVALRY
- **28** ALBUM SPOTLIGHT: *(WHAT'S THE STORY) MORNING GLORY?*
- **30** OASIS VS BLUR … AND LOADS MORE!

26

30

100% UNOFFICIAL

32

40

32 LIVE AND LOUD: GIGS
34 ALBUM SPOTLIGHT: *BE HERE NOW*
36 BEYOND THE HITS
38 ALBUM SPOTLIGHT: *STANDING ON THE SHOULDER OF GIANTS*
40 FASHION FAMOUS
42 ALBUM SPOTLIGHT: *HEATHEN CHEMISTRY*
44 ALBUM SPOTLIGHT: *DON'T BELIEVE THE TRUTH*
46 THE OASIS FAM
48 ALBUM SPOTLIGHT: *DIG OUT YOUR SOUL*
50 STOP CRYING YOUR HEART OUT
52 SOME MIGHT SAY ... OASIS ARE THE BEST BAND IN THE WORLD

42

51

54 INDIE WORDSEARCH
55 I'M OUTTA TIME
56 D'YOU KNOW WHAT I MEAN?
58 PUT YER MONEY WHERE YER MOUTH IS
59 THE MASTERPLAN
60 MUSIC FESTIVAL SUDOKU
62 A – Z OF OASIS
64 ALL AROUND THE WORLD
66 NO CIGARETTES AND ALCOHOL
68 CREDITS
69 ANSWERS

YOU AND I ARE GONNA LIVE FOREVER

Liam Gallagher says Oasis are "the best band on the planet". Let's not argue with him ...

Two brothers. Seventy-five million records sold. Too many fights to count. And a comeback tour that left fans queuing for hours in a clamour for tickets. Bands have come and gone in the 31 years since Oasis released their debut album, **Definitely Maybe**, but they're back where they should be: conquering the world again.

From the heights of playing to a quarter of a million people at Knebworth to their bitter break-up, Oasis are a key part of music history. In the foggy time before the internet, everyone knew what Liam and Noel looked like – and what they were up to – because they were in the newspapers every day. Not just for their music, but for their spats, love lives and controversial one-liners.

Fame was just a dream for these two brothers from Burnage, Manchester, but when they heard The Stone Roses' music they realised they could form a band too. Since the moment they picked up that guitar and tambourine, Oasis have made music that transcends trends: when they started out, the UK was in the middle of a grunge invasion, with Nirvana having their moment. Dance and pop were also massive, alongside pesky fellow indie bands like Blur. But Oasis carried on doing things their way, with one eye on the competition.

Band members come and go, but Liam and Noel are the heart and soul of Oasis. Even when the band were on hiatus, fans could get their fix with Noel Gallagher's High Flying Birds and Liam's Beady Eye. Those bands brought the spirit of Oasis, but they couldn't quite touch the magic that happens when the Gallagher brothers get together.

A love of Oasis unites so many people, from the lads on the football terraces to the girls in their adidas tops – and, of course, politicians, looking for a touch of street cred.

So whether you've been a fan since 1994 or you've just discovered you're mad fer it, let's celebrate the world of Oasis and what they mean to their fans.

FACT FILE

HIT AFTER HIT

Oasis have had eight UK number one hits ... and Wonderwall wasn't one of them:

- **Some Might Say** (1995)
- **Don't Look Back in Anger** (1996)
- **D'You Know What I Mean?** (1997)
- **All Around the World** (1998)
- **Go Let It Out** (2000)
- **The Hindu Times** (2002)
- **Lyla** (2005)
- **The Importance of Being Idle** (2005)

What a drag: Liam and Noel at a press conference

100% UNOFFICIAL

10 MILLION
FANS IN THE ONLINE QUEUE FOR 2025 REUNION TOUR TICKETS

8 UK #1 HITS

26 UK TOP 10 HITS

930 TOTAL WEEKS OASIS ALBUMS SPENT IN THE UK TOP 40

1.4 MILLION TICKETS SOLD FOR 2025 TOUR

Let there be love Knebworth Park, 1996

ROCK 'N' ROLL STARS

Say hello to Our Kid and Our Kid …

ALL THE FACTS ON NOEL DAVID THOMAS GALLAGHER

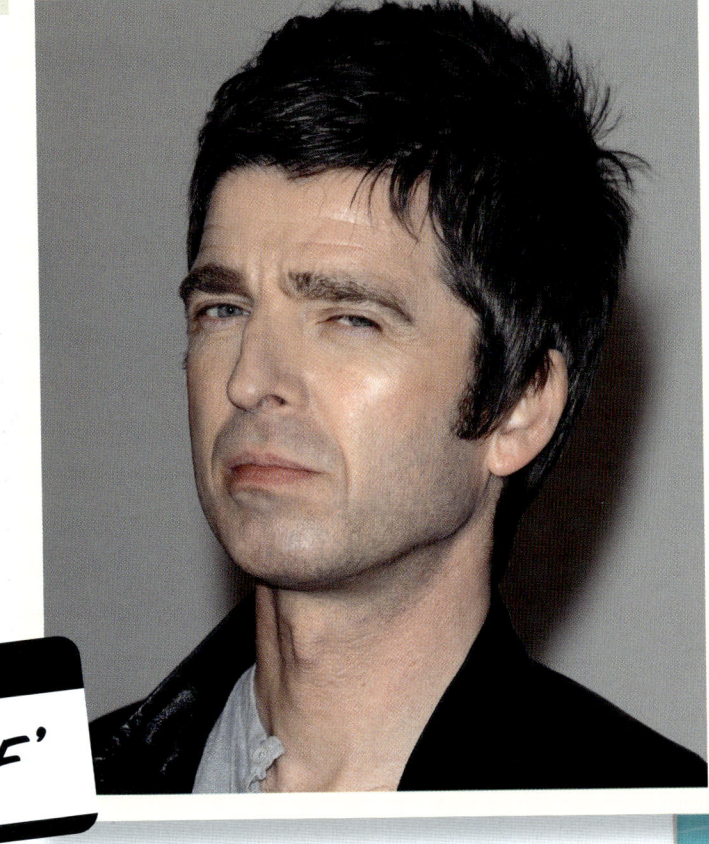

- Noel used to play around with his brother's guitar, so his mum, Peggy, bought him one.

- Noel is left-handed, but plays guitar and eats crisps right-handed.

- Noel left school at 15.

- His first musical love was Irish folk, but then he decided his favourite band was The Smiths.

- At school, Noel called everyone 'chief', but it later became his nickname.

Hello my name is 'CHIEF'

- He got his first taste of tour life as a roadie for Manchester band Inspiral Carpets.

- Not a fan of tattoos, Noel has none.

- Noel used to work at British Gas, where he started to write **Definitely Maybe**.

- Noel says he can't remember meeting David Bowie.

- Despite the Blur vs Oasis chart battle, Noel made up with Damon Albarn and sang backing vocals on Gorillaz' 2017 song **'We Got The Power'**.

NOELS LYRICS

- Noel and his wife Sara MacDonald divorced in 2023 after 12 years of marriage.

- This proud dad says that fatherhood has been one of the great pleasures of his life.

- The first Oasis single Noel sang on was 1996's **'Don't Look Back In Anger'**.

- Noel calls his Gibson 335 guitar from 1960 "a priceless piece of art".

- Despite writing **'Sunday Morning Call'**, Noel says he hates it so much he left it off the singles compilation.

100% UNOFFICIAL

THE LOWDOWN ON WILLIAM JOHN PAUL GALLAGHER
(YES, LIAM'S NOT EVEN HIS REAL NAME!)

- Liam has four GCSEs.

- He donated the profits from his first solo gig to the families of victims of the Manchester Arena bombing.

- Liam claims he lost interest in new music when CDs came out, but likes to have Classic FM on in the background when he's at home.

- Liam has the autoimmune disease Hashimoto's that can affect his voice, so he's a fan of apple cider vinegar.

- If there was a film made of the Oasis story, Liam would like his son Lennon to play him in the early years.

- An early riser, Liam gets up at 5am, then goes for a run.

- Liam says he hasn't voted since he was 18.

Mega Knebworth vibes in the area: 26 years after their legendary Oasis gigs, Liam returned to play a concert without his brother in 2022.

- Despite being able to knock up an excellent stir fry, Liam says cooking "can f*** off." Tell that to his noodles!

- Not just a singer and tambourine player, Liam also has his own clothing label, Pretty Green.

- In 2022, Liam went back to Knebworth, the site of one of Oasis' most legendary gigs, and played solo.

- If Liam could be in any band from history, he'd choose the Sex Pistols.

- When putting together an outfit, Liam likes to start with his shoes and work his way up from there.

- A lifelong Manchester City fan like his brother, Liam loved playing gigs at his favourite team's Maine Road ground – and said Knebworth didn't come close.

- If he wasn't in Oasis, Liam thinks he would have been a labourer.

- Liam adopted two cats, Sid and Nancy, from London's Wood Green Animal Shelter in 2018.

OASIS TIMELINE: 1991-2000

First gigs! Big bust-ups! Even bigger hits! It's your all-important Oasis timeline.

1991

Liam Gallagher, Paul "Bonehead" Arthurs, Paul "Guigsy" McGuigan and Tony McCarroll form the band, The Rain, in Manchester.

Noel Gallagher joins the band and they change their name to Oasis.

August 14 Oasis play first gig, supporting hotly-tipped newcomers Sweet Jesus at Manchester's Boardwalk. Tickets are only £3.

1993

31 May Oasis barge their way onto the bill at Glasgow's King Tut's Wah Wah Hut and Alan McGee, boss of

Creation Records signs them on the spot.

1 July First NME live review. Apparently they were "not perfect". Good though.

21 September Liam's 21st birthday.

30 October Promo of *'Columbia'* released as a white label demo.

1994

27 January Oasis play one of their most important early gigs at the Water Rats in London's Kings Cross.

February Recording of *Definitely Maybe* begins.

18 March First live telly appearance on Channel 4's rowdy Friday night show The Word, playing a speedy version of **'Supersonic'**.

April 'Supersonic' explodes onto the scene – and makes it into the UK top 40.

7 April Liam and Noel argue their way through an interview with NME's John Harris. The recording becomes famous and is even released as a 'bootleg' single.

May Liam goes to a Blur gig in Manchester.

July A historic rock 'n' roll moment dawns as Oasis are banned from London's Columbia hotel, mostly for throwing things out of windows.

29 August release of *Definitely Maybe*.

September Liam hits Noel with tambourine at a gig in San Francisco.

November The band wins Best New Act at the Q Awards.

1995

March 'Some Might Say' video shoot is cancelled after Liam doesn't turn up.

May 'Some Might Say' gives Oasis their first #1 single.

100% UNOFFICIAL

17 April 'Live by the Sea' (a live concert recording) is filmed at the Cliffs Pavilion.

30 April Drummer Tony McCarroll leaves the band.

23 June Oasis headline Glastonbury.

14 August The infamous battle of Britpop: Oasis' new single **'Roll With It'** goes head-to-head with Blur's **'Country House'**.

September Guigsy departs, and band film **'Wonderwall'** video.

2 October Second album **(What's The Story) Morning Glory?** goes straight to UK #1.

December Noel gets a Rolls Royce for Christmas, despite not being able to drive.

1996

19 February Oasis win big at the BRIT Awards.

March Oasis perform not one - but two – songs on legendary music show Top Of The Pops, as **'Don't Look Back In Anger'** goes straight to #1 in the charts.

27-28 April It's a homecoming as Oasis play two nights at Manchester City's Maine Road.

10-11 August Two nights at Knebworth: done!

4 September Liam spits beer and makes rude gestures during a performance of **'Champagne Supernova'** for the MTV VMAs, held in New York.

12 September Rest of the US tour is cancelled, with their record label citing 'internal differences'.

1997

7 April Liam marries Patsy Kensit.

May 29 Police are called to Noel's noisy birthday party at his north London home, Supernova Heights. This was also the day he realised he'd never eaten a boiled egg – an oversight he rectified the next year.

5 June Noel marries Meg Mathews.

21 August Another #1 hit album: **Be Here Now.**

1998

March Bonehead and Guigsy's last gig.

1999

November Gem Archer and Andy Bell join the band.

December Oasis head to Philadelphia to open the **Standing On The Shoulder Of Giants** world tour.

OASIS TIMELINE: 2000-2025

Brawls! More hit albums! Side projects! And that massive comeback ...

2000

January The band's record label is launched: Big Brother Recordings.

7 February Oasis let out **'Go Let It Out'**, giving them another #1 single.

28 February Fourth studio album **Standing On The Shoulder Of Giants** is released.

May Oasis head out to America and Canada on 'The Tour Of Brotherly Love' with US rock band The Black Crowes.

March Pop star Robbie Williams uses his speech at the BRIT Awards to challenge Liam to a televised boxing match.

May On-off, on-off? Noel quits the world tour (but goes back later).

July The band play Wembley, in a gig many fans label as disastrous due to Liam's rambling and swearing.

September Liam and Patsy Kensit divorce.

November Release of first live album **Familiar To Millions**.

2001

January Noel and Meg Mathews divorce.

October Oasis play a mini Noise and Confusion tour, joined by Foo Fighters and friends.

2002

March Bootleg of a new single, **'The Hindu Times'**, is leaked online.

1 July **Heathen Chemistry** gives Oasis another number one album.

March Liam is questioned by police after a ruck outside what was then known as 'London's trendy Met Bar'.

13 July It's fisticuffs *again* for Liam! This time backstage at the Scottish rock festival, T In The Park.

1 August Noel loses his passport just as a US tour begins.

December Liam loses his front teeth during a brawl in a Munich nightclub.

2004

January Drummer Alan White leaves the band.

May Zak Starkey, son of Beatle Ringo Starr, steps in on the drums.

2005

30 May **Don't Believe The Truth**, sixth studio album reaches #1 on release.

22 June It's a biggie: Oasis play New York's famous venue, Madison Square Garden.

14

100% UNOFFICIAL

2006

1 September A pivotal moment in London's nightlife as Liam is banned from the Groucho Club after a tiff with England footballer Paul Gascoigne. Please note: if, like Gazza, you spot Liam eating a bowl of soup, do *not* ask him if we wants a roll with it. Yes, this really happened.

2008

14 February Love is in the air as Liam marries Nicole Appleton.

April Noel claims it's wrong for Jay-Z to play Glastonbury.

September A fan attacks Noel on stage in Ontario, Canada.

6 October Oasis release their seventh, and final, studio album, *Dig Out Your Soul.*

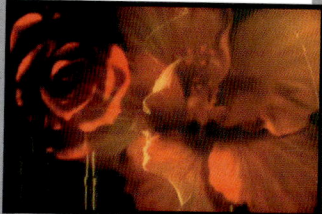

2009

22 August Last gig at Stafford's V Festival.

28 August The Paris Altercation: yes, that fight at Paris' Rock En Seine festival that saw the band split up.

November Liam begins tinkering with new band Beady Eye.

2011

June Noel marries Sara MacDonald but there's no invite for Liam.

July Noel announces a new album, but not with Oasis. Noel Gallagher's High Flying Birds are born.

2016

October The music documentary, 'Oasis: Supersonic' is released.

2024

March Liam goes on tour with The Stone Roses' John Squire and fans love the collaboration.

July Secret photo session featuring both Liam and Noel. What could they be up to?

27 August Oasis announce a long-awaited reunion tour.

31 August Millions bash their heads on their computers trying to buy Oasis tickets.

2025

4 July Oasis start their first tour in over 16 years at Cardiff's Principality Stadium.

LITTLE BY LITTLE

What makes Oasis so great? Let's take a look at their influences ...

THE BEATLES
The Fab Four were a massive influence on Oasis: the haircuts, the chords and the cover versions. But Paul McCartney wasn't impressed by Noel's "We're going to be bigger than The Beatles" posturing. Basically, because no-one is bigger than The Beatles.
LISTEN TO: 'Hey Jude' (You might hear the inspiration behind some of Oasis' riffs.)

THE JAM
Paul Weller's punk pop four-piece ruled the charts in the early '80s, with hits like **'Going Underground'**, **'Start!'** and **'That's Entertainment'**. If you look closely, you'll see Paul and Liam's haircuts have a lot in common – and if you listen closely you'll hear The Jam's frontman adding guitars and backing vocals to **'Champagne Supernova'**.
LISTEN TO: 'The Eton Rifles'

THE STONE ROSES
For a couple of weeks in the summer of 1989, The Stone Roses were the biggest thing in music with their flappy flares and bucket hats. When Noel saw them live, his musical ambitions were sealed. In 2024, guitarist John Squire formed a supergroup with Liam Gallagher and the pair toured to rave reviews.
LISTEN TO: 'Fools Gold'

100% UNOFFICIAL

THE KINKS
Before Oasis, there were two other perma-arguing brothers who stormed the charts: Ray and Dave Davies. With their mod style and musical portraits of old London town, this seminal '60s band were an influence on Liam (not to mention Blur).
LISTEN TO: 'Waterloo Sunset'

THE MOD SCENE
With sharp suits and even sharper barnets (that's hair to those who don't speak Cockney), mods began their cultural rise in the 1950s. By the '60s, they were riding scooters and clashing with rockers on Brighton beach, before taking their place at the centre of Swinging London. Bands like Small Faces (pictured), The Who and later The Jam honed the mod sound and the '60s scene was immortalised in the 1979 film Quadrophenia.
LISTEN TO: 'Lazy Sunday' by Small Faces

INSPIRAL CARPETS
A young Noel was a roadie for the Manchester band, who sprung from the late '80s Madchester scene. They had the bowliest hair and the widest flares, plus some baggy bangers.
LISTEN TO: 'This Is How It Feels'

THE SMITHS
Noel has given his fellow Manchester band (who also enjoyed a good argument or two) props and has covered their classic **'There Is A Light That Never Goes Out'**. Legendary guitarist Johnny Marr has also played with Oasis on several occasions.
LISTEN TO: 'This Charming Man'

THE EARLY DAYS

One small gig. A rowdy but ambitious band. And a record company boss who knew what he liked. The legendary story of how Oasis started out ...

Noel Gallagher said that when he heard The Stone Roses' **'Sally Cinnamon'**, he knew what his destiny was. But at that point, he wasn't yet in Oasis – it was his younger brother Liam's band.

Working as a roadie for Manchester band Inspiral Carpets, Noel was happy to be unleashed from his job at British Gas. The band's Clint Boon says he was an integral part of the Carpets. "He was vital to the development of our band in terms of style, our attitude – he really contributed a lot. His spirit rubbed off on us," he says. Clint did note that Noel liked to get other people to do the hard work!

At this point, the band that would become Oasis were called The Rain, with Liam joined by his mates drummer Tony McCaroll, bassist Paul "Guigsy" McGuigan and Paul Arthurs, AKA Bonehead, on guitar.

The day Noel joined, he insisted they change the name to Oasis, which he took from one of the venues on an Inspiral Carpets tour poster. Liam later told Radio X his early gigs were rubbish because "it was a bit daunting trying to act like Mick Jagger or whatever in front of your mates". He did a cracking job though.

One of their more legendary early gigs was at Glasgow's King Tut's Wah Wah Hut on 31 May, 1993. Little did they know, that Alan McGee, boss of Creation Records which was home to Primal Scream, My Bloody Valentine and Ride, was in the audience.

They had to persuade the promoters to let them on the bill and they only played four songs, including **'Rock 'n' Roll Star'** and a cover of The Beatles' **'I Am The Walrus'**. But it was enough to impress the Scottish music supremo, who changed the brothers' lives by offering them a record deal.

Alan only caught Oasis because his sister made him get to the venue early. "The first song was really good," he recalls. "Then the second was incredible. By the time they did this fantastic version of **'I Am The Walrus'**, I'd decided to sign this group, now." Good idea, mate.

Once other labels got wind of Oasis and their brilliance, they tried to poach them, but the deal was done. The musical landscape of 1993 was ripe for something new and exciting – and Oasis had it by the bucketload.

At this time, grunge bands like Nirvana and Pearl Jam were capturing the cool audience, but it was novelty act, Mr Blobby, who claimed 1993's Christmas number one. The charts *needed* Oasis. And they'd arrived.

It didn't take Noel long to perfect that trademark swagger

Creation boss Alan McGee, the man who signed on the dotted line

100% UNOFFICIAL

THE MASTERPLAN

Liam was OK carrying his microphone, but the tambourine proved too heavy for him

Practising their autographs at this early record store signing.

ALBUM SPOTLIGHT
DEFINITELY MAYBE

IT'S 1994...
The year Pulp Fiction and The Lion King were in the cinema and there was a new toy in town – the Sony PlayStation. Grunge was invading, thanks to bands like Nirvana, but Wet Wet Wet still managed to spend 15 weeks at number one with **'Love Is All Around'**.

"YOU AND I ARE GONNA LIVE FOREVER"
Who loves Noel's guitar solo on **'Live Forever'**? It was originally twice as long, but producer Owen Morris chopped it off because he thought the boys were getting a bit Guns 'N' Roses.

> "*DEFINITELY MAYBE* WAS THE LAST GREAT PUNK ALBUM"
> – NOEL GALLAGHER, WITH A BOLD BUT JUSTIFIED BOAST.

ROCK 'N' ROLL STARS
Radio 1 raved over the rough demo of **'Columbia'**, the track that was originally an instrumental until it was suggested it could do with some lyrics. The song became a tribute to London's most rock 'n' roll hotel, which issued Oasis with a lifetime ban after they threw chairs, tables and a pot plant out of the window.

THE BEST OASIS SONG EVER?
'Slide Away' is one of Noel's favourite Oasis songs and he claims Paul McCartney agrees with him. It doesn't get as many live outings as it should, despite it also being a fan favourite. Noel wrote the song – about his ex-girlfriend - on Johnny Marr's Les Paul guitar and it's about his ex-girlfriend. It was originally intended as a single, but the Gallaghers thought a fifth release from a debut album would be too much.

"MR SIFTER SOLD ME SONGS"
'Shakermaker' is an early classic, with lyrics that might not make sense at first. Liam sang "I've been driving in my car with my friend Mr Soft." But he wasn't talking about his brother. Mr Soft was a character from a Trebor mints advert from the 1980s, which featured a floppy character swaggering along the street. Actually, he walked a bit like Liam. And Mr Sifter was from a record shop in Didsbury, Manchester, which is now home to an Oasis mural.

"YOU GOTTA MAKE IT HAPPEN"
Definitely Maybe was re-released in 2024, with bonus outtakes and unreleased demos and went straight back to number one in the album charts. Half the sales were on vinyl, proving that both new and old fans still had an appetite for the classic album.

OTHER ALBUMS OUT THIS YEAR:
Nirvana: **MTV Unplugged in New York**, Blur: **Parklife**, The Manic Street Preachers: **The Holy Bible**, Beastie Boys: **Ill Communication**, Beck: **Mellow Gold**, TLC: **CrazySexyCool**, East 17: **Steam**, Madonna: **Bedtime Stories**.

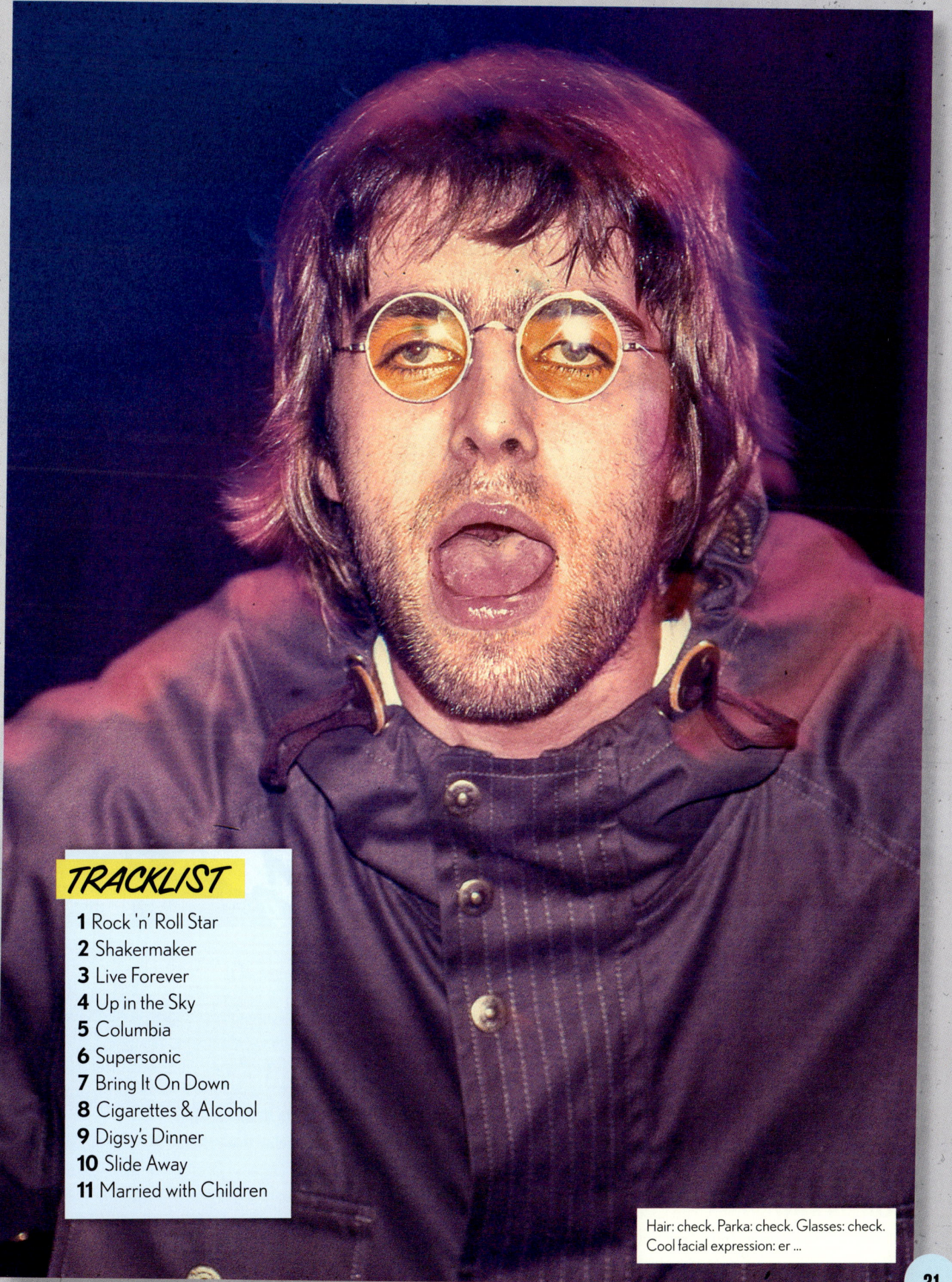

100% UNOFFICIAL

TRACKLIST

1 Rock 'n' Roll Star
2 Shakermaker
3 Live Forever
4 Up in the Sky
5 Columbia
6 Supersonic
7 Bring It On Down
8 Cigarettes & Alcohol
9 Digsy's Dinner
10 Slide Away
11 Married with Children

Hair: check. Parka: check. Glasses: check. Cool facial expression: er …

COOL BRITANNIA

The year is 1995. East 17's 'Stay Another Day' is still in the charts. Toy Story is showing at the cinema. Oasis are getting ready to release *(What's the Story) Morning Glory?* And Britpop's moment is now, thanks to these superstars.

BLUR
By the time Oasis signed their first record deal in 1993, Blur were already on their second album. The band brought floppy hair, cockney cheer and **Girls & Boys** to Britpop.
BIGGEST BANGER: Parklife
BRITFACT: Blur were originally known as Seymour.
OASIS SAY: Lots. Liam described Blur as "Chimney sweeping music".

SUPERGRASS
At the more bouncy end of Britpop were three young scamps from Oxford who burst onto the scene with their debut album, *I Should Coco*. They are Oasis-adjacent having supported the band on the **Be Here Now** tour in 1997.
BIGGEST BANGER: Alright
BRITFACT: The band were turned into long-armed muppets for the video for their 1999 hit **Pumping on Your Stereo**.
OASIS SAY: Nothing. The Gallaghers have no beef with Supergrass. Phew!

ELASTICA
Britpop queen Justine Frischmann formed Elastica after leaving Suede – and she took the spotlight as frontwoman. The three-quarters female Elastica specialised in short, punky pop songs and although their time was brief they exported Britpop to the US too.
BIGGEST BANGER: Waking Up
BRITFACT: Blur's **Tender** is written about Justine, who dated Damon Albarn (Blur) and Brett Anderson (Suede).
OASIS SAY: "Her music is beyond uninspiring" – Noel, on Justine. Brutal!

100% UNOFFICIAL

SUEDE

Oasis didn't invent the 'make great album, break up, get back together' technique: Brett Anderson and Bernard Butler had already done it by the height of Britpop. Butler walked out for good during the recording of second album **Dog Man Star**, Suede carried on and in 1995 they played the Phoenix Festival with Bob Dylan (when tickets cost a paltry £25).
BIGGEST BANGER: Trash
BRITFACT: Comedian Ricky Gervais was their manager in the early days!
OASIS SAY: When asked if Suede would be supporting them on tour, Liam Gallagher tweeted: "Not happening there too cocky esp that singer" [sic].

THE VERVE

Richard Ashcroft's band had been knocking around since the early '90s, but their 1995 album **A Northern Soul** established them as one of Britpop's finest. Oasis supported them in the early days, before the tables turned. Richard Ashcroft is a firm friend of the Gallaghers and they chose him to support them on their 2025 reunion tour.
BIGGEST BANGER: Bitter Sweet Symphony
BRITFACT: The **Bitter Sweet Symphony** video was inspired by trip hop band Massive Attack's **Unfinished Sympathy** – and it inspired Fat Les' novelty football anthem **Vindaloo**.
OASIS SAY: "I loved touring with them. I just remember Ashcroft having his socks and shoes off" – Liam.

PULP

Sheffield band Pulp brought artiness to pop, with Jarvis Cocker's trademark specs and lyrics about misfits, babies and the meaning of life. Their album **Different Class** summed up 1995 like no other, from having no money in the supermarket to partying in fields. The most theatrical band of the time, Jarvis made the headlines for one of his most iconic moments - when he invaded the stage and wiggled his bum during Michael Jackson's overblown performance of **Earth Song** at the 1996 BRIT Awards.
BIGGEST BANGER: Common People. Or is it **Disco 2000**?
BRITFACT: Pulp were originally called Arabicus, a spelling mistake Jarvis found in the Financial Times. Clever.
OASIS SAY: "I thought Pulp were great people and they had one or two great tunes, but we had 12" – Noel.

OASIS: OFF THE CHARTS!

You might think the band reached their peak in the mid-'90s, but 30 years later they're as huge as ever.

8 UK NUMBER ONE SINGLES

8 UK NUMBER ONE ALBUMS

FIRST UK TOP 40 SINGLE: 'SUPERSONIC' (APRIL 1994)

22 UK TOP TEN SINGLES IN A ROW

FIRST UK NUMBER ONE: 'SOME MIGHT SAY' (MAY 1995)

1475 WEEKS IN THE UK TOP 75 ALBUM CHART

250,000 PEOPLE WATCHED THEM OVER TWO NIGHTS AT KNEBWORTH IN 1996

MOST STREAMED OASIS SONG: 'WONDERWALL' – 400 MILLION STREAMS AND COUNTING

16 YEARS IN THE UK TOP 75 ALBUM CHART

OASIS HAVE HAD THREE HITS ON AMERICA'S BILLBOARD CHARTS

100% UNOFFICIAL

1 LAST NUMBER ONE:
'THE IMPORTANCE OF BEING IDLE' (2005). UNLESS THERE'S MORE TO COME …

THE BAND INITIALLY ANNOUNCED 14 STADIUM DATES IN THE UK AND IRELAND, BUT THAT GREW TO **41 DATES ACROSS THE GLOBE**

14 MILLION PEOPLE TRIED TO GET TICKETS FOR THE 2025 TOUR

THE ULTIMATE ACHIEVEMENT:
OASIS ARE ONE OF THE FEW BANDS TO HAVE PLAYED TWO SONGS ON ONE EPISODE OF TOP OF THE POPS — 'Don't Look Back In Anger' and its B-side 'Cum On Feel The Noize' in 1996

30 YEARS AFTER THEIR FIRST SINGLE, OASIS WERE THE MOST GOOGLED MUSIC ACT OF 2024

'How to get Oasis tickets' was the top 'how to' question of the year.

IN 1996 KNEBWORTH TICKETS COST **£22.50**

IN 2025 TICKETS STARTED AT **£75**

SPOTIFY
REPORTED A **690%** INCREASE IN STREAMING OF OASIS SONGS AFTER THEY ANNOUNCED THEIR 2025 TOUR

BE HERE NOW
SOLD **696,000** COPIES IN ITS FIRST WEEK OF RELEASE, AUG '97

THE 2025 TOUR IS RUMOURED TO NET THE BAND **£400 MILLION**

BY 2025, OASIS HAD SOLD **75 MILLION** RECORDS WORLDWIDE

DON'T LOOK BACK IN ANGER

Eyebrows: check. Coats: check. Noel and Liam are serving looks.

It's not all brotherly love, let's explore Liam and Noel's biggest beefs.

YOU WHAT? *1994*
In a legendary interview with NME, insults fly about getting kicked off ferries, footy hooligans and smashing up studios.

CLANG! *1994*
Noel flees their American tour and Liam throws a tambourine at his head.

THWACK! *1995*
Noel cracks Liam over the head with a cricket bat during a row in the recording studio.

BYE! *1996*
Liam pretends to lose his voice and walks out of Oasis' MTV Unplugged. Then finds it again to heckle Noel's performance.

UH-OH! *2000*
Noel quits the tour in Barcelona after Liam made a comment about his daughter, Anais.

CIAO! *2005*
Oasis are playing a festival in Italy when Liam wanders off stage in the middle of **Champagne Supernova**.

AU REVOIR! *2009*
Noel finally quits the band after a big ruck at a Paris festival.

CHEERS! *2010*
Liam thanks everyone in the band at the BRIT Awards. Except Noel.

RUDE! *2011*
Liam renames Noel's band 'The High Flying Turds'.

SPUDDY! *2016*
Liam posts several photos of Noel on Twitter and captions them various versions of 'Potato'.

PROTEIN! *2016*
Liam claims Noel didn't turn up to the Supersonic movie premiere because he's at home eating tofu.

MEAN! *2017*
Noel doesn't play Manchester's One Love benefit gig. Liam is not impressed with his brother's no-show.

TEARS! *2017*
2017: Liam calls Noel's tears at his Manchester Arena benefit gig "a PR stunt".

100% UNOFFICIAL

WIBBLING RIVALRY

Shades at the ready: it's a Liam vs Noel quote-off.

Liam is ready for the pouting contest.

LIAM ON NOEL

"OUR KID LOOKS MORE LIKE LOUIS WALSH THESE DAYS."
LIAM'S BROTHERLY LOVE, AS ALWAYS.

"HE'S A PRICK, HE'S TURNED INTO THE MIDDLE CLASS. HE'S TURNED INTO THE ESTABLISHMENT. HE'S ONE OF THEM. HE'S ALL F***ING, LIKE, MR PRIM AND PROPER."
MIND YOUR LANGUAGE, LIAM!

"WHEN I THINK ABOUT IT, BEING IN A BAND WITH HIM BORES THE DEATH OUT OF ME."
LIAM WAS LOOKING FORWARD TO THE REUNION

"HE'S THE ANGRIEST MAN YOU'LL EVER MEET. HE'S LIKE A MAN WITH A FORK IN A WORLD OF SOUP."
FOOD FOR THOUGHT FROM NOEL

"IT'S MADE HIM PULL HIS FINGER OUT AND WORK FOR A LIVING AT LAST."
NOEL ON LIAM'S SOLO CAREER

"... HE SOUNDS LIKE ADELE SHOUTING INTO A BUCKET ..."
NO, HE REALLY DOES

NOEL ON LIAM

Noel knows what it's all a-pout ...

27

ALBUM SPOTLIGHT
(WHAT'S THE STORY) MORNING GLORY?

IT'S 1995...
DJ Chris Evans was hosting the BBC Radio 1 Breakfast Show, PJ Harvey wowed Glastonbury in a pink catsuit and Wonderbra (with some fabulous songs) and London bands were hanging out at Camden's The Good Mixer pub. Kate Moss was dating Johnny Depp and People Magazine crowned Brad Pitt the sexiest man alive.

ROLL WITH IT
This was the first song the band recorded for the album – who were recording at Rockfield Studios in Wales – and the one that made the cut was only the second take. It was new drummer Alan White's first day in the studio.

> "WHILST **DEFINITELY MAYBE** IS ABOUT DREAMING OF BEING A POP STAR IN A BAND, **WHAT'S THE STORY** IS ABOUT ACTUALLY BEING A POP STAR IN A BAND"
> – NOEL, NAILING THE FEELING OF OASIS' GOLDEN ERA.

WONDERWALL
It's one of the band's defining songs, but was kept off the number one spot in the UK singles chart by cheesy crooners Robson & Jerome's **I Believe**. Noel wanted to do a lead vocal on the album, so he gave Liam the choice of **Wonderwall** and **Don't Look Back In Anger**. Legend has it Noel was pretty chuffed when Liam chose **Wonderwall**, leaving him with the song he wanted.

"HELLO, HELLO, IT'S GOOD TO BE BACK..."
(What's The Story) Morning Glory? became the fastest-selling album of all time, after Michael Jackson's **Bad**. It stayed in the top three of the album chart for seven whole months.

(WHAT'S THE STORY) MORNING GLORY?
Helicopters! Drugs! Swaggering guitars! This song gave the album its title, but **(What's The Story) Morning Glory?** came from a phrase a woman Noel met in America used to say. He thought it was a common greeting, a bit like 'Top of the morning', and was surprised to discover it wasn't. But he liked it enough to name an album after it.

CAST NO SHADOW
The last song written for the album, Noel describes **Cast No Shadow** as "a f***ing great song" with "some of the best words I ever wrote" in it. Which is entirely accurate. He doesn't remember writing it though. At the time, The Verve had been going through one of their many fall-outs, so Noel dedicated the song to Richard Ashcroft.

OTHER ALBUMS OUT THIS YEAR:
Pulp: **Different Class**, Radiohead: **The Bends**, Blur: **The Great Escape**, No Doubt: **Tragic Kingdom**, Alanis Morissette: **Jagged Little Pill**, The Chemical Brothers: **Exit Planet Dust**, Coolio: **Gangsta's Paradise**, Lighthouse Family: **Ocean Drive**, Robson & Jerome: **Robson & Jerome**

100% UNOFFICIAL

TRACKLIST

1 Hello
2 Roll with It
3 Wonderwall
4 Dont Look Back in Anger
5 Hey Now!
6 Untitled (Swamp Song Version 1)
7 Some Might Say
8 Cast No Shadow
9 She's Electric
10 Morning Glory
11 Untitled (Swamp Song Version 2)
12 Champagne Supernova

Find someone who looks at you like Noel looks at his favourite Epiphone guitar

OASIS VS BLUR ... AND LOADS MORE!

The summer of 1995 saw a fierce chart battle when two of the finest Britpop bands went head-to-head in the charts. But that's not the only ruck Oasis were involved in ...

THE MOST FAMOUS FEUD OF ALL

All hell broke loose in 1995 when Blur and Oasis released singles on the same day – 15 August. The NME called it 'The Big Chart Showdown', with Blur's **Country House** facing off Oasis' **Roll With It**. Before that, the two bands had kept their distance, but the press whipped up a 'no-nonsense north' vs 'arty south' divide that did nobody's record sales any harm.

Blur's single was a novelty romp that featured scantily-clad women in the video, while Oasis went for a straightforward stadium anthem that Noel called "a simple rock 'n' roll tune." There was definitely room for both, but as the release date got nearer a war of words erupted. Noel made a 'joke' about hoping Damon Albarn and Alex James would die and later backtracked. In 2020, Liam cleared up rumours that the feud was sparked by romantic rivalry on X. "Just for the record me and Dermot Oblong never fell out over a girl or boy ..." Glad he cleared that one up. Damon later said: "Oasis were like the bullies I had to put up with at school." Reports of stolen dinner money haven't been confirmed or denied.

As fans rushed to HMV and Our Price stores to hand over their £2.99 for the song, those sales totals looked close, but Blur pipped Oasis to the number one slot. Oasis sold an impressive 216,000 copies of **Roll With It**, but Blur's **Country House** sold 274,000. Alex James claims: "Blur won the battle, Oasis won the war, then Blur went on to win the whole campaign." But maybe it's not over yet ...

Blur vs Oasis: Calm down, Our Kid, they're friends again now, actually

"CALM DOWN, OUR KID"

100% UNOFFICIAL

Other targets for Liam and Noel's tongue lashings ...

ROBBIE WILLIAMS
The Gallaghers were mates with Robbie when he left Take That and they hung out at Glastonbury in '95. But Robbie has also described them as "gigantic bullies" after Noel called him the "fat dancer from Take That" at the 2000 BRIT Awards. Mean.

"Come and join Take That, you handsome fella!"

MUSE
Liam doesn't hate the rockers in principle, but he does seem to have a problem with lead singer Matt Bellamy, who he finds 'creepy'. "They at least play guitars, but when I hear his voice I'm like, 'F*** him,'" he says. Matt remains unbothered by the criticism.

LEWIS CAPALDI
Noel piled in on Lewis, saying: "Chewbacca should enjoy his 15 minutes." Lewis refused to be drawn into the beef, wearing a T-shirt with Noel on at Glastonbury 2019.

Matt B: Getting on with his job and ignoring Liam's harsh words

'Chewbacca' showing his love for Noel

GREEN DAY
Liam took aim at Billie Joe Armstrong, saying: "I just don't like his head." His head did not reply.

KEANE
"Squares," said Noel. Bit harsh!

Billie Joe and his head. Quite likeable, actually. Pointless feud!

Keane: Are they 'squares' or do they just enjoy a nice early night?

LIVE AND LOUD: GIGS

The summer of 1996 saw Oasis swagger into the big league of stadium fillers.

Imagine a time before smartphones. When people watched gigs instead of filming them for TikTok. When parents hammered the landline to pay for their kids' gig tickets by cash or cheque. When tickets cost £17.50 in the north and £22.50 in the south.

That time is 1996 and Oasis were at the height of their live powers (when aren't they?). When the band announced two nights at Knebworth, playing to more than 250,000 people, two and half million tried to get tickets.

At their first big stadium show at Manchester City's Maine Road in April, the 80,000 strong crowd were treated to support from Manic Street Preachers and Ocean Colour Scene. If you, (or your mum or dad) have a souvenir ticket and you're wondering why Bonehead is missing from the photo on it, that's because he's a Manchester United fan and

Was this the exact moment when an unimpressed Oasis saw the size of the Knebworth guestlist?

100% UNOFFICIAL

Knebworth Liam: "Who wants to drive the backstage golf cart?" Noel: "Me, meeeee!"

Loch Lomond We're not saying the catering was bad at Loch Lomond, but Liam got so peckish he ate his tambourine

Maine Road A big gig at Maine Road brought the band closer to their beloved Manchester City

refused to be on it! He did turn up to the gig though. Liam nearly didn't, if you believe rumours that there was a kidnap plot targeting him just before the big day.

In August, Oasis played to 80,000 people in a spectacular setting on the banks of Loch Lomond, transforming a small Scottish town into, well, an oasis of fans. Support came from Black Grape, Ocean Colour Scene, Cast, The Bootleg Beatles and Heavy Stereo (Gem Archer's previous band).

Then came Knebworth. Thousands of people were on the guest list, including DJ Chris Evans, supermodel Kate Moss and Ant and Dec. The celebs were given Oasis-branded binoculars to watch the show. The band whizzed around on golf buggies and looked like they were having the time of their lives.

Noel says he can't remember walking on stage at Knebworth, but even fans with the most patchy memories can recall every minute. Saturday saw The Prodigy, Manic Street Preachers, Ocean Colour Scene, The Chemical Brothers and The Bootleg Beatles warm up the crowd. On Sunday, the Manics were joined by Kula Shaker, Cast and Dreadzone. When The Charlatans took to the stage, it was only a few weeks after their keyboard player Rob Collins had died in a car accident, so Primal Scream's Martin Duffy stood in.

Oasis opened both days at Knebworth with **Columbia**, **Acquiesce** and **Supersonic**, as they did at their Loch Lomond gig the previous week. They played the same set both nights.

These big outdoor gigs defined the swaggering spirit of Oasis and their fans in 1996. Arms aloft, cagoules everywhere and adidas trainers firmly stamped on once the bouncing got going, these were glorious days that still make fans who were there a little misty-eyed.

33

ALBUM SPOTLIGHT
BE HERE NOW

IT'S 1997 ...

Labour's Tony Blair won the election, The English Patient was at the cinema and squeaky kids' favourites the Teletubbies were on the telly. Kids and adults were reading Harry Potter. Britpop and bucket hats were everywhere. Dolly the sheep was cloned. And the world was shocked when Princess Diana died in a car crash in Paris.

D'YOU KNOW WHAT I MEAN?

The opening track of **Be Here Now** was as bold and brash as the Gallaghers. By now, the brothers were tabloid favourites and Noel arrived at Tony Blair's Downing Street party in a Rolls Royce. The single knocked Sheryl Crow off the #1 spot as fans clamoured for a taste of their new album.

"MY BIG MOUTH, MY BIG NAME ..."

In 2017, Liam Gallagher told NME that **Be Here Now** was his favourite Oasis album, giving it a solid ten out of ten. "The only problem is our kid thought he'd be a bit of a producer, whereas a producer would have gone: 'Leave it out with them Slash guitars, mate', 'This song's a bit long'. That's why Noel hasn't got fond memories of it. But I think it's f***ing class," he said. Fans note that they did just fine without a producer.

ALL AROUND THE WORLD

One of Noel's criticisms of **Be Here Now** is the length of the songs. Packed with guitar wibbles, the songs are longer than those on previous albums, with **'All Around The World'** coming in at more than nine minutes. The Verve's Richard Ashcroft supplies backing vocals and it was the longest number one single the UK charts had ever seen.

"AT THAT TIME, WE THOUGHT IT WAS F***ING GREAT, IT JUST WASN'T MORNING GLORY" - LIAM
– AND WHO ARE WE TO ARGUE?

"FOREVER AND A DAY ..."

Both Gallagher brothers got married in 1997: Noel tied the knot with Meg Mathews in Las Vegas and Liam and Patsy Kensit plumped for a traditional wedding at London's Marylebone Town Hall. This was also the year that Liam and Patsy posed in bed under a Union Jack duvet for Vanity Fair's cover to celebrate swinging London.

"SO WHAT'S THE MATTER WITH YOU? SING ME SOMETHING NEW ..."

After **(What's The Story) Morning Glory?**, Knebworth and a chaotic tour of the US, Oasis headed back into the studio to make another album. Liam had been in the habit of not turning up to gigs and preferred to go house-hunting with Patsy Kensit, who he was about to marry. "I don't like it as a record," says Noel. "But I loved it at the time." Millions of fans agree.

OTHER ALBUMS OUT THIS YEAR:
Radiohead: **OK Computer**, Wu-Tang Clan: **Wu-Tang Forever**, The Verve: **Urban Hymns**, Daft Punk: **Homework**, Mariah Carey: **Butterfly**, Spice Girls: **Spiceworld**, U2: **Pop**, Supergrass: **In It For The Money**, The Prodigy: **The Fat Of The Land**, Backstreet Boys: **Backstreet's Back**, Michael Jackson: **Blood On The Dancefloor**, Foo Fighters: **The Colour And The Shape**

TRACKLIST

1 D'You Know What I Mean?
2 My Big Mouth
3 Magic Pie
4 Stand By Me
5 I Hope, I Think, I Know
6 The Girl in the Dirty Shirt
7 Fade In-Out
8 Don't Go Away
9 Be Here Now
10 All Around the World
11 It's Gettin' Better (Man!!)
12 All Around the World (Reprise)

100% UNOFFICIAL

"Backstreet's back ... alright! Oops, sorry, might have got the wrong album there"

BEYOND THE HITS

A deep dive into the Oasis back catalogue. How many do you have?

COMPILATION ALBUMS

FAMILIAR TO MILLIONS (2000)
Recorded at Wembley during a wibbly time, this live album is still a corker

KNEBWORTH 1996 (2021)
In 2021, this snapshot of Oasis at their peak was released, with a documentary too

DEFINITELY MAYBE: SINGLES (1996)
This box set is a must for collectors, with early singles and demos

(WHAT'S THE STORY) MORNING GLORY? SINGLES (1996)
Covers, singles, b-sides and a storming Glasto performance of **'Live Forever'**

THE MASTERPLAN (1998)
You want b-sides that are so good they should have been singles? Oasis have got 'em by the bucketload, as showcased by this compilation

STOP THE CLOCKS (2006)
Noel had a tough job picking out the songs for this semi-greatest hits collection

TIME FLIES ... (2010)
A whopping 27 singles from Supersonic to Falling Down. If you want the greatest hits, here they are

SINGLES

1994
- Supersonic
- Shakermaker
- Live Forever
- Cigarettes and Alcohol
- Whatever

1997
- D'You Know What I Mean?
- Stand By Me

2000
- Go Let It Out
- Who Feels Love?

2003
- Songbird

2007
- Lord Don't Slow Me Down

2009
- Falling Down

1995
- Some Might Say
- Roll With It
- Wonderwall

1998
- All Around The World

2002
- The Hindu Times
- Stop Crying Your Heart Out
- Little By Little/She Is Love

2005
- Lyla
- The Importance Of Being Idol
- Let There Be Love

2008
- The Shock Of The Lightning
- I'm Outta Time

100% UNOFFICIAL

NOTABLE B-SIDES

TALK TONIGHT, ACQUIESCE
These beautiful **'Some Might Say'** b-sides have had many airings and are always a treat if you hear them live.

ROCKIN' CHAIR
On the flip of **'Roll With It'** and a proper singalong too.

HALF THE WORLD AWAY
Made famous as the theme tune to '90s comedy The Royle Family, this was the other side of **'Whatever'**.

THE MASTERPLAN
The king of Oasis b-sides, as heard on **'Wonderwall'**.

STEP OUT
A little too close to Stevie Wonder's **'Uptight (Everything's Alright)'** to make it onto *(What's The Story) Morning Glory?*, but great as a b-side to **'Don't Look Back In Anger'**.

ROUND ARE WAY
Not a great example of spelling but a live favourite, as seen on **'Wonderwall'**.

CUM ON FEEL THE NOIZE
Talking of lack of spelling skills, this cracker of a Slade cover is found on **'Don't Look Back In Anger'**.

FADE AWAY
The stomping b of **'Cigarettes And Alcohol'** that could have been a hit single.

MY GENERATION
A romp through The Who fave on the other side of **'Little By Little/She Is Love'**.

STAY YOUNG
An optimistic and bouncy singalong found on the flip side of **'D'You Know What I Mean?'**.

(IT'S GOOD) TO BE FREE
An early b-side (**'Whatever'**) that has a little bit of the *Be Here Now* sound about it.

ALBUM SPOTLIGHT
STANDING ON THE SHOULDER OF GIANTS

IT'S 2000...
Or Y2K, as it was also known. The world had a narrow escape from the Millennium Bug, Denise Lewis won big at the Olympics and England had a disaster at Euro 2000. Kylie Minogue was **'Spinning Around'** in gold hotpants, **'Who Let The Dogs Out?'** by the Baha Men ruled the charts and there was a new reality show on telly called Big Brother.

STANDING ON THE WHAT?
The album's title comes from the phrase Noel spotted on a £2 coin in a pub. (It's actually 'shoulders', but we're not going to argue.) The year 2000 was a difficult time in Oasis world, with Bonehead and Guigsy leaving the band a year earlier. It was rumoured Guigsy quit in the most '90s way possible – by fax.

GO LET IT OUT
The first single from **Standing On The Shoulder Of Giants** was **'Go Let It Out'**. With no Guigsy, Oasis hadn't yet found a replacement so Noel played bass in the video, which features Liam smirking on a double decker bus while the rest of the band hang around waiting for him. Written by Noel, it's classic Oasis: deliciously Beatles-esque and full of lyrics that nearly make sense. It knocked Gabrielle's long-running **'Rise'** off the top spot in the UK charts, only to be replaced by All Saints' **'Pure Shores'** after one week.

WHERE DID IT ALL GO WRONG?
In the late '90s, Noel's mansion, Supernova Heights, in London's Belsize Park, was *the* place to be at that time. He hosted legendary parties, while paparazzi waited outside trying to snap celebrities such as Kate Moss coming out in the early hours. Noel wrote **'Where Did It All Go Wrong?'** just before he and then-wife Meg Mathews sold it in 1999.

LITTLE JAMES
Liam claims he wrote **'Little James'** in three minutes after playing around with the tune. It's about Patsy Kensit's son. The couple's divorce was finalised the same year this album came out and Liam moved on to date Nicole Appleton from All Saints.

"ORDINARY PEOPLE THAT ARE LIKE YOU AND ME"
Two new members joined the band: Ride's Andy Bell and Gem Archer, who was in Heavy Stereo. Fascinating fact: Gem is the only musician who's played in Oasis as well as both Liam and Noel's solo projects, Beady Eye and High Flying Birds. This was a turbulent year for Oasis as Liam appeared in a highly refreshed state at their Wembley gig.

> "ALL THE LYRICS TO THAT ALBUM ARE AMAZING"
> – NOEL, IN AN UNCHARACTERISTICALLY MODEST MOOD.

OTHER ALBUMS OUT THIS YEAR:
Coldplay: *Parachutes*, Eminem: *The Marshall Mathers LP*, Linkin Park: *Hybrid Theory*, Robbie Williams: *Sing When You're Winning*, Doves: *Lost Souls*, Craig David: *Born To Do It*, S Club 7: *7*, Backstreet Boys: *Black and Blue*, Kylie Minogue: *Light Years*, Radiohead: *Kid A*, Britney Spears: *Oops!...I Did It Again*

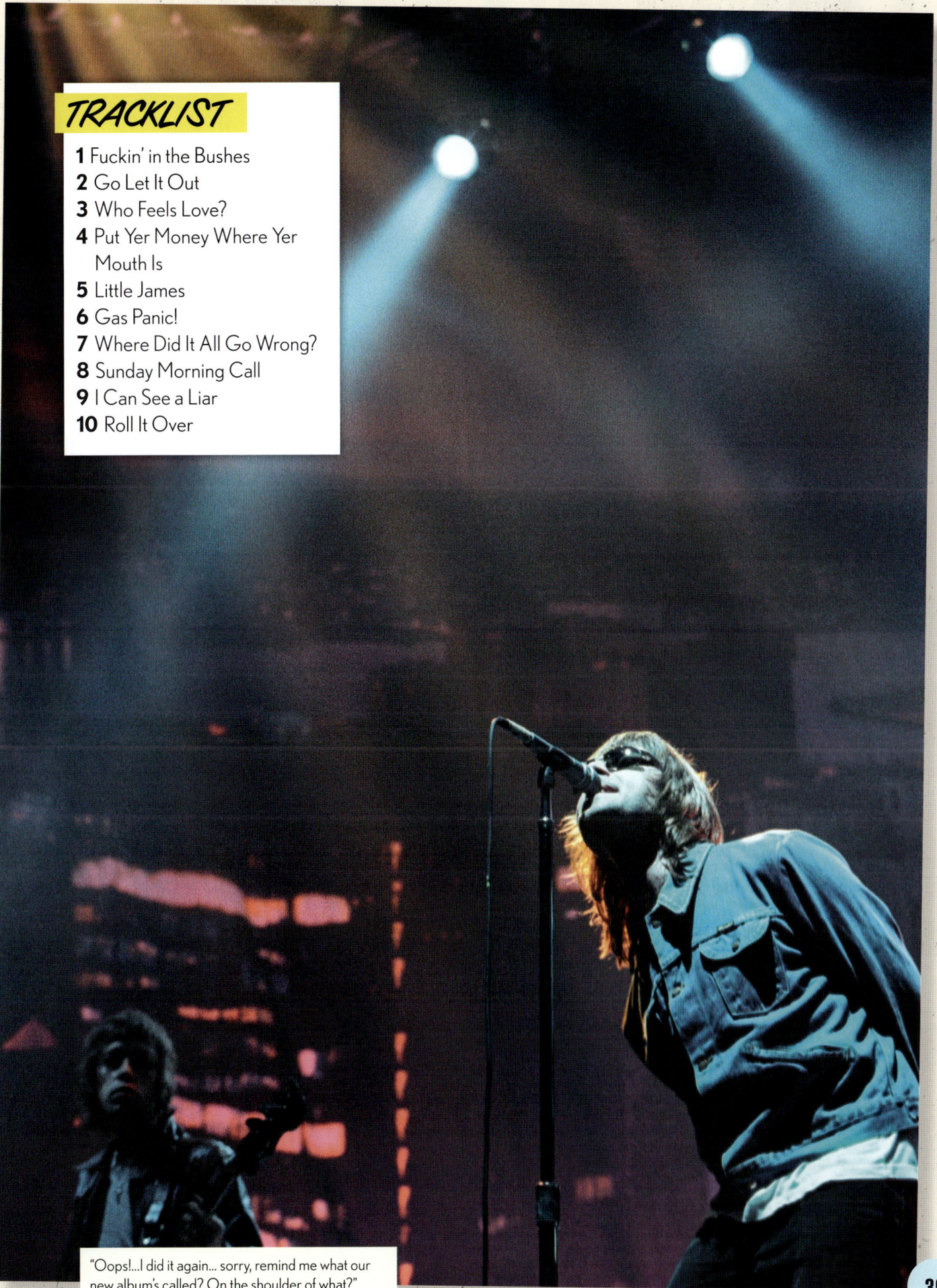

TRACKLIST

1. Fuckin' in the Bushes
2. Go Let It Out
3. Who Feels Love?
4. Put Yer Money Where Yer Mouth Is
5. Little James
6. Gas Panic!
7. Where Did It All Go Wrong?
8. Sunday Morning Call
9. I Can See a Liar
10. Roll It Over

"Oops!...I did it again... sorry, remind me what our new album's called? On the shoulder of what?"

FASHION FAMOUS

From bucket hats to adidas trackies, Liam and Noel's style remains evergreen ...

LIAM'S BAKER BOY HAT (2005)
Bad hair day or fashion statement? This sixties-style cap is ideal for those days when Liam doesn't fancy showing his face.

In 2025, Liam's hat would have its own TikTok stan page.

THE COSY PARKA (1996)
Both Liam and Noel know the power of a parka for looking cool and keeping out the cold.

Liam and Noel: er, can anyone remind us where we're from again?

JOHN LENNON SPECS (1996)
The Beatles are a key influence, right down to Liam's glasses which are giving Lennon ... or is it Potter?

UNION JACK CHIC (2001 AND 1996)
It's a little bit mod and a little bit retro – Liam's not afraid to model one of the band's key motifs on his jacket. Noel may not have the jacket, but he does have the Union Jack guitar.

Harry Potter and the Liam of Sunshiiine ...

100% UNOFFICIAL

A NOD TO SPORTSWEAR (2011)
Noel brings his own brand of cool to the humble jumper with a mod-esque stripe.

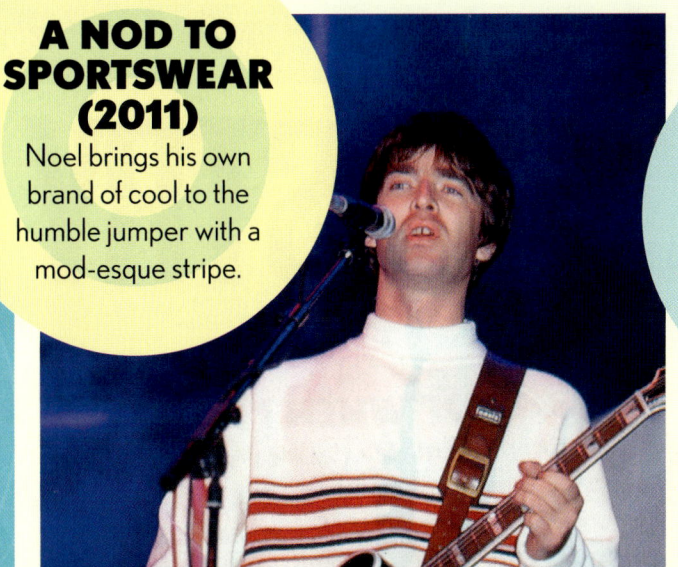

Noel looking sportier than Sporty Spice on sports day in a sports car. Sort of…

THE FRED PERRY (1996)
Neither shirt nor T-shirt, the iconic polo is a hit with Oasis and their fans.

BROTHERS IN LEATHER (1998)
Leather jackets are a perennial Gallagher favourite, as modelled here by Noel and Liam.

Beer bottle: model's own.

BUCKET HAT (1996)
In a nod to The Stone Roses, Liam has a bigger collection of bucket hats than Noel has guitars.

Liam and his Kangol bucket hat. Home to hair, cash, drinks … it's like a Tardis in there!

SIXTIES STYLE (2001)
Liam's not afraid to experiment with high fashion, as he demonstrates in a little faux fur number.

"And then they said: 'You got a roll with it.' Nearly spat out my soup, Our Kid!"

41

ALBUM SPOTLIGHT
HEATHEN CHEMISTRY

IT'S 2002...
Pop Idol fever gripped the nation, with Will Young battling Gareth Gates for pop supremacy (and winning). Sisters Venus and Serena Williams also faced a battle in the Wimbledon final. Three years after their festival debut, Coldplay headlined the main stage at Glastonbury. And some people had tiny mp3 players that could hold 500 songs. Ah, they'll never catch on …

"I GET UP WHEN I'M DOWN …"
Heathen Chemistry was the first album Oasis made without a producer and the whole band were on writing duties. At one point, Liam had Henry the Hoover mic'ed up for a special effect, but Noel decided to get rid of it in case fans started chucking Hoovers up on stage. The album's title comes from a T-shirt Noel bought in a second-hand shop.

"WE LOST IT, BUT WE DEFINITELY GOT IT BACK. A LOT OF THAT'S TO DO WITH FRESH MEMBERS IN THE BAND"
– NOEL, FEELING INVIGORATED BY A LINE-UP CHANGE.

STOP CRYING YOUR HEART OUT
This year had its ups and downs for Oasis: they played triumphant outdoor gigs at London's Finsbury Park and Ireland's Witness Festival. The US tour was less successful and Noel and Andy were taken to hospital after a car crash in Indiana. Liam, meanwhile, lost his front teeth in a brawl in a Munich hotel bar and had to be bailed out by management.

SONGBIRD
Clocking in at just over two minutes, Liam wrote this song about his fiancée, All Saints' Nicole Appleton. Their son Gene was born the year before this album was released. **'Songbird'** was the first song written by Liam to get into the UK singles charts, peaking at number three. He claims he wrote it in ten minutes and Noel loved it because it was so simple.

HUNG IN A BAD PLACE?
Online music review site, Drowned In Sound, claimed **Heathen Chemistry** was smothered in "big, dumb rock moves and dated, boring, unoriginal arrangements." The Guardian branded it "Yawning glory". NME didn't mince their words, saying it had: "droning raga-guitars, the occasional screech of feedback and the most garbled lyrics since Magic Pie". Um, OK. But wait – some of the fans are very fond of it!

LITTLE BY LITTLE
Oasis' first double A-side single was **'Little By Little'** and **'She Is Love'**. Noel wanted both of them to be released as he liked them so much; and **'Little By Little'** remains one of his – and their fans' – favourites. Actor and friend of Oasis Robert Carlyle, best known at the time for his role in Trainspotting, plays a small man in the video.

OTHER ALBUMS OUT THIS YEAR:
The Streets: **Original Pirate Material**, Coldplay: **A Rush Of Blood To The Head**, Foo Fighters: **One By One**, Daniel Bedingfield: **Gotta Get Thru This**, Sugababes: **Angels With Dirty Faces**, Avril Lavigne: **Let Go**, The Libertines: **Up The Bracket**, Chemical Brothers: **Come With Us**, Liberty X: **Thinking It Over**, Nelly: **Nellyville**, Red Hot Chili Peppers: **By The Way**, S Club Juniors: **Together**

42

"Stop crying your heart out ... see, at least one of us knows the words, Liam"

100% UNOFFICIAL

TRACKLIST

1 The Hindu Times
2 Force of Nature
3 Hung in a Bad Place
4 Stop Crying Your Heart Out
5 Songbird
6 Little by Little
7 A Quick Peep
8 (Probably) All in the Mind
9 She Is Love
10 Born on a Different Cloud
11 Better Man

ALBUM SPOTLIGHT
DON'T BELIEVE THE TRUTH

IT'S 2005...
Video game Guitar Hero was released, TV viewers were hooked on Lost and Harry Potter And The Goblet Of Fire was at the cinema. In the news, London was hit by the 7/7 bombings, Prince Charles married Camilla Parker Bowles and a general election gave Labour another term in power. And it was a very soggy Glastonbury headlined by The White Stripes, Coldplay and Basement Jaxx.

> "I'VE REDISCOVERED THE SPARK TO ACTUALLY WRITE SONGS AGAIN, INSTEAD OF TRYING TO SUM UP THE MEANING OF LIFE IN FIVE MINUTES. WE'LL LEAVE THAT TO COLDPLAY. THEY KIND OF DO IT BETTER THAN ANYBODY ELSE"
> – NOEL, DISHING OUT THE PRAISE TO CHRIS MARTIN.

LYLA
When drummer Alan White departed, the Gallaghers brought in a sticksman with a heavyweight pedigree, which is how Zak Starkey, son of Beatle's drummer Ringo Starr, came to drum on **'Lyla'**. Noel has said the song is about the excitement of being in a new relationship and it could be about Sara MacDonald, who he met in Ibiza in 2000. They married in 2011. Although he has joked that Lyla is the sister of Sally from **'Don't Look Back In Anger'**.

"KEEP THE DREAM ALIVE"
When Oasis played Cardiff's Millennium Stadium, they were joined by Razorlight, The Coral and Foo Fighters in a line-up they billed Noise and Confusion. Where are those Foo Fighters now, eh? Even NME praised the gig, which mixed beloved classics with newer songs and B-sides.

THE IMPORTANCE OF BEING IDLE
It was Notting Hill meets Burnage when actor Rhys Ifans starred in the video for this black and white video. He plays a dancing undertaker about to witness his own funeral and Liam and Noel are his bosses. Kylie Minogue fans might be surprised to read the video was directed by Dawn Shadforth, who also did the iconic **'Can't Get You Out Of My Head'**.

"THE SUN WILL SHINE ON YOU AGAIN"
This album gave Oasis their final two number one hits, with **'Lyla'** and **'The Importance Of Being Idle'**, and went triple platinum in the UK. **Don't Believe The Truth** went to number one in the UK, Argentina and Japan.

"A MAN'S GOT A LIMIT"
With Alan leaving the band and Liam and Noel claiming they didn't speak to each other in an interview with US music magazine Spin, things weren't great in the Oasis camp in 2005. But the boys would live to fight another day – and make another album ...

OTHER ALBUMS OUT THIS YEAR:
Kaiser Chiefs: **Employment**, Hard-Fi: **Stars Of CCTV**, Gorillaz: **Demon Days**, The Pussycat Dolls: **PCD**, Charlotte Church: **Tissues And Issues**, McFly: **Wonderland**, Coldplay: **X&Y**, Gwen Stefani: **Love. Angel. Music. Baby**, Bloc Party: **Silent Alarm**, Daft Punk: **Human After All**, Mariah Carey: **The Emancipation Of Mimi**, James Blunt: **Back To Bedlam**, Jamiroquai: **Dynamite**

"You're beautiful, it's true. Oh no, hang on, that's Blunty, isn't it?"

100% UNOFFICIAL

TRACKLIST

1. Turn Up the Sun
2. Mucky Fingers
3. Lyla
4. Love Like a Bomb
5. The Importance of Being Idle
6. The Meaning of Soul
7. Guess God Thinks I'm Abel
8. Part of the Queue
9. Keep the Dream Alive
10. A Bell Will Ring
11. Let There Be Love

THE OASIS FAM

Take a look at Liam and Noel's family tree, from WAGS to kids …

MEG MATHEWS
MARRIED TO NOEL 1997–2001

Noel and Meg – the subject of Wonderwall – tied the knot in Las Vegas, but had an expensive divorce when daughter Anais was a baby.

Noel's ex-wife Meg, conveniently posing by a Wonderwall.

ANAÏS GALLAGHER
BORN 2000

Noel and Meg's level-headed daughter who's making a name for herself in film. She even went online to defend younger Oasis fans who were making old men grumpy by snapping up tickets for the reunion tour.

Anais, daughter of Noel and Meg and an all-round good egg!

SARA MACDONALD
MARRIED TO NOEL 2011–2023

Noel and Scottish PR boss Sara met in Ibiza and hit it off. They have two sons together, Donovan and Sonny.

DONOVAN AND SONNY GALLAGHER
BORN 2007 AND 2010

Noel's lookalike sons with Sara are teenagers, but will they inherit their dad's musical genes? Time will tell …

Sara and Noel in happier times … and sparklier ones.

GENE GALLAGHER
BORN 2001

Liam and Nicole's son Gene has modelled for adidas and is also forging a career as frontman of indie band Villanelle, who've supported his dad on tour.

Gene: as that wise prophet of pop Charli xcx says, the apple don't fall far from the tree.

NICOLE APPLETON
MARRIED TO LIAM 2008-2014

All Saints' singer and DJ, Nic married Liam on Valentine's Day, but when Liam told her he'd had a daughter, Gemma, by American journalist Liza Ghorbani (just before it hit the newspapers), they separated.

All Saints' Nicole styling it like The Beatles in her red jacket.

GEMMA GALLAGHER
BORN 2013

You don't see much of Gemma in the public eye ... yet.

100% UNOFFICIAL

PATSY KENSIT
MARRIED TO LIAM 1997-2000

The model, singer and actress posed with Liam for an iconic Vogue cover in one of their finest moments. They have one son, Lennon.

Lennon with mum Patsy: model mum, model son.

LENNON GALLAGHER
BORN 1999

With his mum's model genes it's no surprise Liam's lookalike son Lennon is making a career out of being a model for Burberry, Lanvin and Saint Laurent, plus following in his dad's footsteps as a musician.

MOLLY MOORISH-GALLAGHER
BORN 1998

With a rock star for a dad (Liam) and a singer for a mum (Lisa Moorish), Molly was destined for fame. She's an Instagram influencer and model.

Liam and Lisa's little Molly: grown up and destined for fame.

ALBUM SPOTLIGHT
DIG OUT YOUR SOUL

IT'S 2008...
The UK came last in the Eurovision Song Contest, which was won by Russia. Cheryl Cole joined The X Factor judging panel, replacing Sharon Osbourne – and it was the year that Alexandra Burke beat JLS. In EastEnders, Bianca and Rickaaaay returned to Albert Square. And Britney Spears made her comeback, with sixth album, Circus.

"WE ARE THE VICTIMS OF OUR OWN BRILLIANCE"
– NOEL GALLAGHER. WELL, WHO ARE WE TO ARGUE?

"DIG OUT YOUR SOUL, 'COS HERE WE GO"
The album was originally going to be called **'Bag It Up'**, but perhaps the Gallaghers remembered Geri Halliwell had already used the song title in 2000. They were stuck for an album title, so *Dig Out Your Soul* came from a line in **'To Be Where There's Life'**, written by Gem.

FALLING DOWN
Noel was shocked when a man attacked him onstage at a festival in Toronto in 2008. The drunken fan shoved him onto the speakers, leaving him with broken ribs. Incredibly, he managed to finish the gig before being taken to hospital. "My first thought was: 'Why me? Why not him? Why not the other fella? I'm writing all the tunes here, mate,'" he said. Liam got off lightly there.

"I'M OUTTA TIME"
Often described as one of the most underrated Oasis albums, *Dig Out Your Soul* went to number one in the UK charts and stayed in the top 40 for 13 weeks. **'I'm Outta Time'** sees Liam Gallagher on songwriting duties, in a reflective mood with its black and white video. It features a sample of one of John Lennon's last interviews from 1980.

"TELL THE WORLD YOU LOVE THEM IN A MELODY"
Dig Out Your Soul was a real collaborative effort. The album was recorded in the legendary Abbey Road Studios, with most songs written by Noel Gallagher, except three by Liam and one each by Gem Archer and Andy Bell. They even got to go to The Beatles' echo chamber and twang on the sitar.

"HOLD THE LINE"
Was *Dig Out Your Soul* predicting Oasis' break-up? **'Falling Down'**, written by Noel, includes the lines: 'Time to kiss the world goodbye' and 'We are a dying dream', while the album closes with a message to 'soldier on'. And of course there's Liam's message that 'I'm outta time'. Less than a year later that prophecy came true.

OTHER ALBUMS OUT THIS YEAR:
Coldplay: **Viva La Vida**, Beyoncé: **I Am... Sasha Fierce**, Lady Gaga: **The Fame**, Katy Perry: **One Of The Boys**, Hot Chip: **Made In The Dark**, Adele: **19**, MGMT: **Oracular Spectacular**

Liam and Noel, united for in sweet harmony for now, but there'd be drama round the corner …

100% UNOFFICIAL

TRACKLIST

1 Bag It Up
2 The Turning
3 Waiting for the Rapture
4 The Shock of the Lightning
5 I'm Outta Time
6 (Get Off Your) High Horse Lady
7 Falling Down
8 To Be Where There's Life
9 Ain't Got Nothin'
10 The Nature of Reality
11 Soldier On

STOP CRYING YOUR HEART OUT

The torturous tale of Oasis' last gig before their 2009 break-up.

Is that Liam modeling the leather jacket that broke a million hearts? Nice, isn't it?

100% UNOFFICIAL

The Paris Altercation. Le Grande Ruck. The fight to end all fights. Call it what you want, but 28 August 2009 is etched in the collective consciousness of Oasis fans as a dark day for their favourite band.

Of course, the band had always been volatile, whether that was Liam's jibes at his brother, Noel goading Liam, or that time one of the brothers threw a tambourine at the other's head. (Naming no names, Liam.)

Noel had quit the band before, in the middle of their world tour in 2000, but he came back. It was Liam's turn to throw a tantrum in 2005 when he walked off stage during **'Champagne Supernova'**.

But the band had always patched things up. This time was different. There'd been tension for weeks and Liam and Noel preferred to travel separately so they didn't have to speak to each other.

Nearing the end of the tour, they were booked to play Rock En Seine in Paris, weeks after cancelling their second night of the V Festival in Chelmsford because Liam had laryngitis. Rumour had it that Noel was annoyed about Liam promoting his Pretty Green clothing firm – and he reached his limit when he witnessed his bro arguing with Bonehead over a leather jacket.

Backstage in Paris, Liam began to wield a guitar like an axe and – already on the edge – Noel didn't find his brother's antics funny. Five minutes before they were about to go on stage, Noel decided he didn't want to go on.

Bloc Party's Kele Okereke informed the crowd of the no-show, with a touch of sarcasm as he announced Bloc Party were now headlining.

"We are never ever getting back together ... until 2025, obviously"

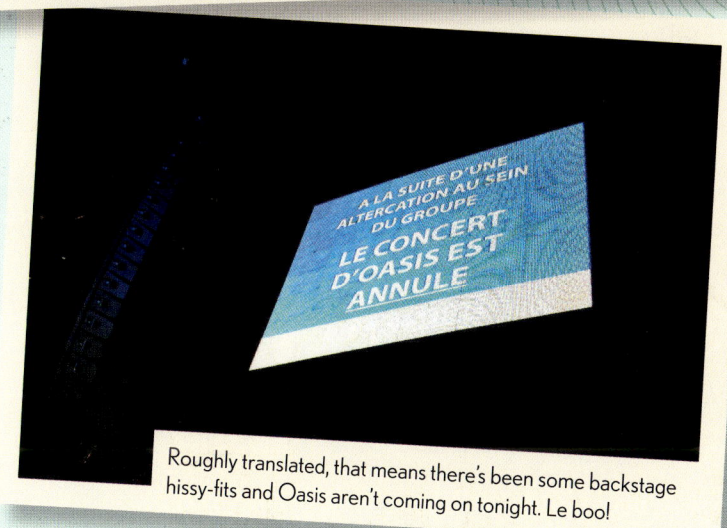

Roughly translated, that means there's been some backstage hissy-fits and Oasis aren't coming on tonight. Le boo!

Many fans assumed it was a joke, but when a message beamed onto the stage saying: "As a result of an altercation within the band Oasis gig is cancelled" they realised it was serious.

Noel said he couldn't go on working with Liam "a day longer" and it looked like the band would never get back together again.

Then in 2013 Noel quashed reunion rumours and when they did the rounds again two years later both brothers denied them. Fans lost hope when Liam began to refer to Noel as a potato on social media, but found it again when he wished him a happy 50th birthday.

Although Noel told Jonathan Ross he'd do a reunion for £100 million, no-one offered him the cash. But when Blur reformed there was a glimmer of hope that Oasis might reignite their old rivalry.

So 16 years later, after solo projects, guest vocals and a war of words (plus many reassurances to fans that a reunion would never be on the cards) Oasis once again embarked on a world tour in 2025.

SOME MIGHT SAY … OASIS ARE THE BEST BAND IN THE WORLD

What do today's pop stars think of the Gallaghers? The reviews are in …

The least Oasis can do is cover Chappell Roan's Good Luck, Babe! live to return the compliment

CHAPPELL ROAN
In 2023 Chappell downgraded the Oasis anthem **'Champagne Supernova'** to **'Red Wine Supernova'** on her debut album *The Rise And Fall Of A Midwest Princess*. Although she wasn't born when the original came out, Chappell is proud of her nod to the band, telling Glamour magazine her song was like "lesbian Oasis".

ARIANA GRANDE
Coldplay's Chris Martin shared a beautiful moment with the Wicked star at One Love Manchester when he serenaded her with **'Don't Look Back In Anger'** and she sang along.

SKY FERREIRA
Liam was spotted sitting next to Sky in the front row of a Saint Laurent show at Paris Fashion Week in 2015 and she responded to reports of an Oasis reunion on social media with: "!!!!!!" A true stan.

KENDRICK LAMAR
Although Kendrick's love for Oasis is clear – he wore the band's **'Live Forever'** T-shirt on tour – Liam preferred to keep fans guessing when they asked if he'd join the star on stage at the Superbowl.

Kendrick Lamar: Going Supersonic in Sweden

100% UNOFFICIAL

BLOSSOMS
Famed for hanging out with Rick Astley, the Stockport band have previously supported Noel Gallagher's High Flying Birds. "We've never shied away from saying how much they've (Oasis) influenced us," singer Tom Ogden told NME. "We went to watch them at Heaton Park when we were 16." How to make a band feel old.

Blossoms: inspired by Oasis, but not by their barbers

LOUIS TOMLINSON
Noel might not have any love for One Direction, but the feeling isn't mutual. Louis admitted he was gutted to miss out on reunion tickets. "I grew up loving the likes of Arctic Monkeys and Oasis," he says. Louis will be pleased to hear that Liam gave him props on X, saying he's a "top lad". Lovely!

Louis: "Shout out to anyone who can get me Oasis tickets"

ENTER SHIKARI
The boys covered **'Half The World Away'** at their live gigs and singer Rou Reynolds told Louder mag he was a 'Britpop kid. "The first album I bought was Oasis. I specifically remember buying **Be Here Now**," he says. "They were the first big band I got into and I bought all their albums. I was drawn to the big songs and Noel Gallagher's amazing songwriting."

SUKI WATERHOUSE
Model-turned-singer Suki is another star who's covered **'Don't Look Back In Anger'**. She admitted the crowd at California music festival Coachella weren't that into it, but when she tried it again at London's All Points East the crowd joined in for a mass singalong.

Enter Shikari: The former Britpop kids showing love for Oasis

Dave Grohl: "I wanna hear those Oasis fans right now. I say: 'Super', you say: 'Sonic'"

FOO FIGHTERS
Dave Grohl teamed up with Liam at the Taylor Hawkins tribute concert for **'Rock 'n' Roll Star'** and **'Live Forever'**. As a long-term campaigner for an Oasis reunion, Dave described Liam as "one of the few last remaining rock stars", but Noel advised him to "wind his neck in" because the band were never getting back together. Needless to say, Dave had the last laugh.

53

INDIE WORDSEARCH

Think you're mad fer Oasis? See how long it takes you to find all forty words in this word search.

WORD LIST:

ACOUSTIC
ALBUM
ANTHEM
BRITPOP
BROTHERS
BUCKET HAT
COOL BRITANNIA
CREATIO
CROWD
FESTIVAL
FIGHT
GUITAR
HEADLINERS
ICONIC
KNEBWORTH
LEGENDS
LES PAUL
LIAM
MADCHESTER
MODS
MUSIC
NINETIES
NOEL
NUMBER ONE
OASIS
OUTSPOKEN
PARKA
RECORDS
REUNION
RIVALS
ROADIE
ROCKERS
SONGWRITING
STAGE
SUPERNOVA
HEIGHTS
SWAGGER
TAMBOURINE
TOUR
TRAINERS
UNION JACK

```
D U A A W G L Y D H D J B C S A M J R C A C O U S T I C J C
A V M X R E U E C O Z R U S E A H A M G J G T U R Q Z G O E
O A T O U T S P O K E N C L I I I J L B A A U A P D D U Y U
X R L U A H L P G B W B Q L A Y Y A I N N A T I R B L O O C
J H V S T A G E M V K Y Y C F E S T I V A L A S W O X O U O
M O Q S S U K P H Y Z N E D H G U C D H B O H B H M M A T Z
T P B M D K T P L A U Z C S T S S M W P Q M C B Y H R S E E
S R L F L R S G B Q D I M M R H R D O P A R K A U B U I R D
X S A A P N O Q U O L U V E N U M R E G G A W S K J M S O A
V R R I L N B C I I S N K E O F S J P A N T H E M H L R T R
Y A Q X N S O H E I T C Q T U Z S B Z J E O M U U S T Y T C
U G C F I E K Z C R O A R T R Y R O A D I E X H Z O O Z J U
V E R E L O R G D R N M R P W U X X X D Z Y N N V U N T B F
E N O U N R C S H L K O Q I C O N I C G S O Y U I D D C J R
E I W C I J J Y U B E Z D I K M W S S P D N Q P X A Q T Z V R
M R D C N R N C G O Y S G T S T H G I E H A V O N R E P U S
A U F G E U S L P N E Q K C A J N O I N U N M H A H B B Z J
D O C V T V D E R W Q L D W Q E L U Y P N O Q S P C Y R P Q
C B J T I V N P G F B M D D Y Q R Z R X S E B L H O H O N E
H M K L E S E A H Q U X T B Y H W C X M O K D A F C E T R W
E A Z R S L G Y L D W R B W Z Y Y N H I V B F A H W Q
S T B P O Y E L G U N U M B E R O N E Y G M W I P I D E Y M
T H U K V S L E H J R K D I C A Q Z I B W W T R O G L R X S
E B C Q V R M S G D D N R L Q Q U X B R E P J X H I S O C
R D K P T O L P G B G Q L B S T C Q K C I I V L H T N F C O
J Q E I J B E A P D I X U T Y N C A L L T V T Y V A E C U Q
M L T B Z R K U J Z D M Y N O I N U E R I S M P M W R Y F H
T B H U H H W L G R A H K Y O N Q W G R N F P K O N S S N U
O K A D B R P W T F T C C F T Q V Z R A G B A G I P J G N D
G B T O K F F K H Q G P P S S H T R O W B E N K M P R V G E
```

54 ANSWERS ON PAGE 69

I'M OUTTA TIME

100% UNOFFICIAL

How quickly can you work out these tricky anagrams of Oasis song titles? We've made it easy by only using song titles from Definitely Maybe and (What's the Story) Morning Glory?

CANDID HERMIT WHIRLER

LONGING MORRY

HAKES REMARK

LOTTI WHIRL

DAISY WALE

NERD WALLOW

FIRE REVOLVE

A COWHAND TOSS

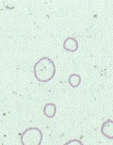

BIND GROWN INTO

CAVEMAN HANGUP POSER

ANSWERS ON PAGE 69

55

D'YOU KNOW WHAT I MEAN?

Definitely Maybe broke the British record as the fastest selling debut album and was recently re-released to celebrate its 30th anniversary. It has sold a reported 8 million copies worldwide. If you haven't heard most of these songs then we will assume you live under a rock.

What was that sound ringing around your brain? Can you match these cryptic descriptions to the songs?

1. ROCK 'N' ROLL STAR

A — SLIDE INTO MY DMS, I THINK WE'LL SHINE!

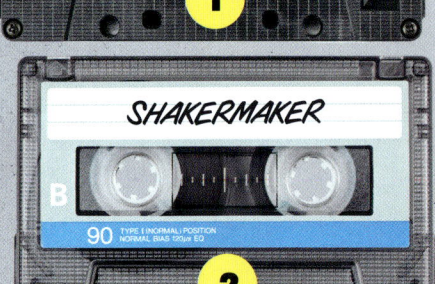
2. SHAKERMAKER

B — TWO UNHEALTHY THINGS THAT YOU REALLY SHOULDN'T INDULGE IN ...

3. LIVE FOREVER

C — GIN AND TONIC AND BMWS AND YELLOW SUBMARINES AND ALKA-SELTZER ...

4. UP IN THE SKY

D — WATCH OUT, HIGH FLIERS AND TREE CLIMBERS, YOU MIGHT FALL DOWN!

5. COLUMBIA

E — DELICIOUS PASTA DISH ON THE MENU TONIGHT!

100% UNOFFICIAL

SUPERSONIC — 6

F — CONCERNED WITH IMMORTALITY.

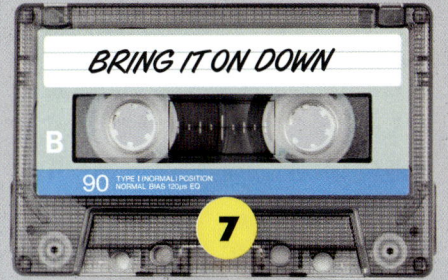
BRING IT ON DOWN — 7

G — THE BOOKS YOU READ AND THE MUSIC YOU LISTEN TO, ARE REALLY NOT TO MY TASTE …

CIGARETTES & ALCOHOL — 8

H — THROWBACK TO MR SOFT, MISTER CLEAN AND MISTER BENN.

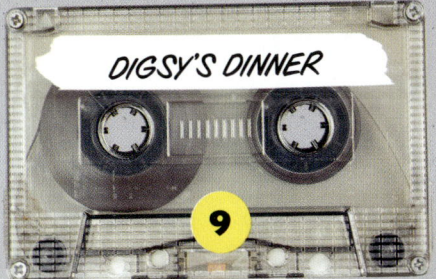
DIGSY'S DINNER — 9

I — THAT FEELING WHEN YOU HEAR RINGING? IT MIGHT BE BECAUSE YOU PUT YOUR HEAD IN A FISH TANK …

SLIDE AWAY — 10

J — CITY-DWELLER DREAMING OF SUNSHINE AND BIGGER THINGS.

MARRIED WITH CHILDREN — 11

K — THERE'S A LOT OF CONFUSION AROUND NEW FEELINGS

ANSWERS ON PAGE 69

PUT YER MONEY WHERE YER MOUTH IS

How well have you paid attention to the facts in this book? See if you can put these iconic Oasis gigs in correct date order.

OASIS — MAINE ROAD, MANCHESTER

OASIS — KING TUT'S WAH WAH HUT, GLASGOW

OASIS — MADISON SQUARE GARDEN

Rock En Seine

CARDIFF PRINCIPALITY STADIUM

OASIS — KNEBWORTH

Oasis — Cliffs Pavilion, Southend-on-Sea

TOUR OF BROTHERLY LOVE

ANSWERS ON PAGE 69

THE MASTERPLAN

100% UNOFFICIAL

Are you a rock 'n' roll star? Or will you be looking back in anger? Test your knowledge of the band with this crossword.

ACROSS
4. Location of the Oasis Leisure Centre (6)
6. Liam's fave Oasis album (2,4,3)
7. Hotel that Oasis was banned from in '94 (8)
9. The Beatles song most covered by the band (1,2,3,6)
11. Original band name (3,4)
12. Fellow headliners on the Noise and Confusion tour (3,8)
13. Make of Johnny Marr's guitar on which Noel wrote Slide Away (3,4)
17. Iconic London studio where Dig Out Your Soul was recorded (5,4)
18. Tracks 6 and 11 on (What's the Story) Morning Glory? (5,4)
19. One of the confirmed support acts for Oasis Live '25 (4)

DOWN
1. Alan, owner of Creation Records (5)
2. Paul Arthur's nickname (8)
3. First UK Number 1 for the band (4,5,3)
5. Oasis' most streamed song (10)
7. First stop on Live '25 World Tour (7)
8. Rival band that nabbed the Number 1 in Aug '95 (4)
10. Site of iconic gigs in '96 (9)
14. Mancunian band that inspired Noel to make music (5,5)
15. Famed (usually muddy) music festival Oasis headlined in '95 (10)
16. City location of the band's demise (5)

ANSWERS ON PAGE 69

MUSIC FESTIVAL SUDOKU

How do you pass the time when waiting for your favourite band to come on stage? By playing music festival Sudoku, of course! Complete each grid by drawing in the correct picture (or just writing the number), in each square. Every line and column must only contain one of each picture.

1   **2**   **3**

4   **5**  **6**

7   **8**   **9**

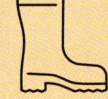  

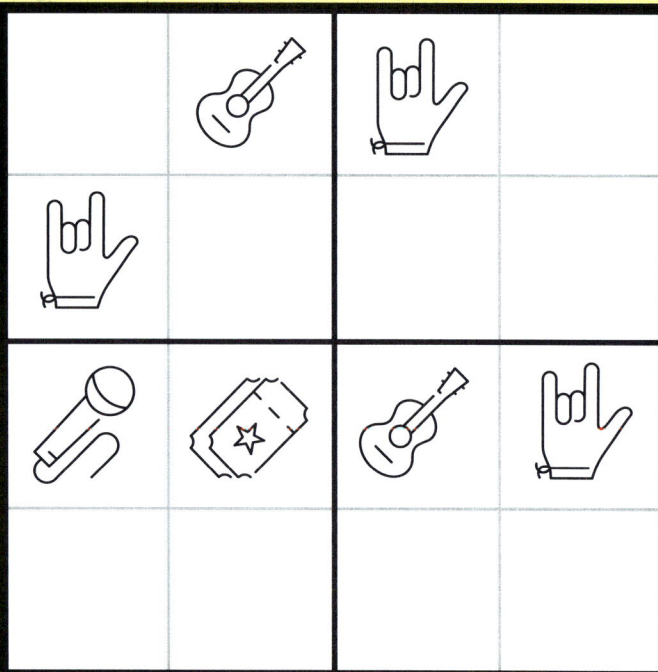

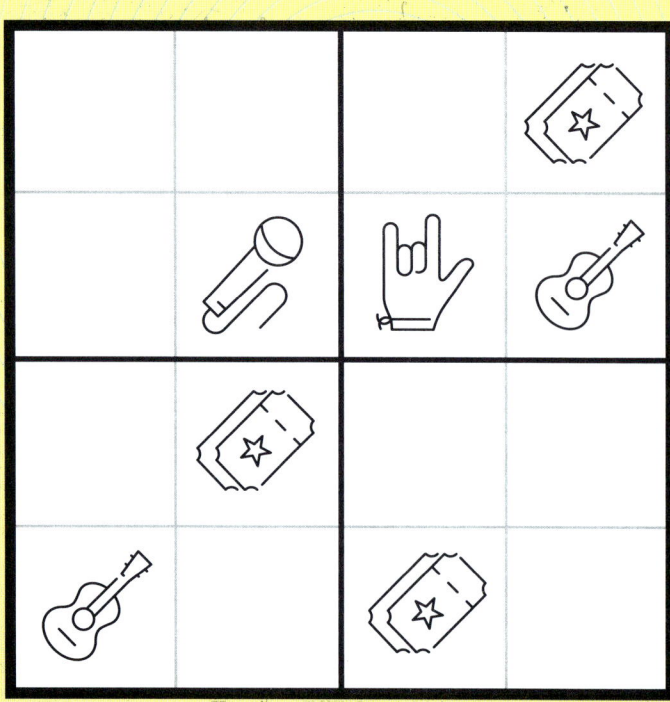

100% UNOFFICIAL

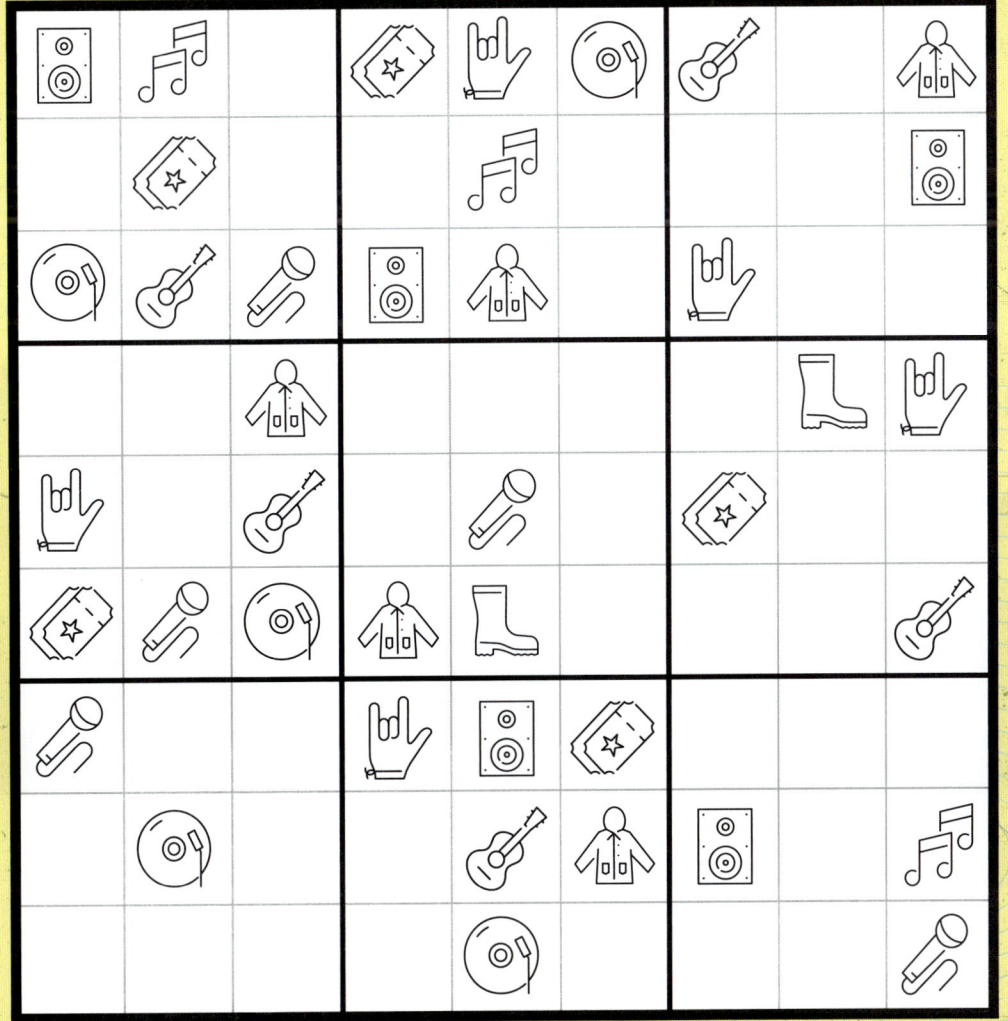

ANSWERS ON PAGE 69

61

A - Z OF OASIS

A dictionary of the Gallaghers, from Awards (there have been many) to Zoo (home of two very naughty penguin chicks).

A – AWARDS, if there's a music award that Oasis haven't either won or been nominated for, then we're yet to hear about it. Brit, Ivor Novello, Mercury Prize, MTV, NME, Q ... they must have a really big cabinet at home!

B – (THE) BEATLES, let's face it, most British guitar bands have been inspired by these legends.

C – CIGARETTES AND ALCOHOL, the quintessential indie anthem of the 1990s.

D – DEFINITELY MAYBE, broke the British record for the fastest-selling debut album, definitely iconic!

E – EXITS, Oasis were certainly not short of members exiting the band over the years, including Liam and Noel. Hopefully their new 2025 line-up will be the winning combo!

F – FOOTBALL, both Noel and Liam are lifelong supporters of Manchester City F.C.

You might spot Liam and Noel in the stands on match day.

G – GALLAGHER, PEGGY Before Liam and Noel there was Peggy, their mum. It is rumoured she was the one who finally succeeded in convincing her boys to reconcile. Thanks Peggy!

H – HECKLING, something the brothers often did to one another, naughty!

I – I AM THE WALRUS, the famed cover of The Beatles' hit that cemented Alan McGee's decision to sign the band.

J – JOHNNY MARR, guitarist of The Smiths, loaned Noel the Les Paul guitar on which 'Slide Away' was written. Thanks Johnny!

K – KNEBWORTH, the band broke the UK record for biggest gig, with a 125,000-strong crowd each night.

Knebworth: most of these people are on the guestlist.

L – LASAGNE – 'Digsy's Dinner' is rumoured to be a cheeky swipe at rivals Blur. This classic pasta dish obviously inspired Noel.

A TO Z OF OASIS

100% UNOFFICIAL

M – "MAD FER IT" – a phrase repeated up and down the land by fans, as Oasis-fever and the Madchester scene took hold.

N – NINETIES, some might say this was the best decade for British music (since the Swinging Sixties), but maybe we're biased!

O – OASIS, no, not the band, the Oasis Leisure Centre in Swindon, of course. The unlikely inspiration for the band's early name change.

P – PRETTY GREEN, Liam's clothing line. We'll take a T-shirt, Liam!

Q – Q AWARDS 2000, the scene for yet another round of insults, this time between Liam and Robbie Williams.

Liam was feeling smug picking his Scrabble letters.

R – REUNION – Oasis Live '25 is the tour that everyone was hoping for, even if only the very lucky ones that actually bagged tickets.

S – SUPERNOVA HEIGHTS, Noel's House. The 'coolest pad in London' according to NME.

T – TAMBOURINE, Liam's accessory of choice on-stage for those percussion solos.

Liam: "T is for tambourine ... and tantrums"

U – UNDER THE INFLUENCE, Noel is on record as stating demo record 'Columbia' was recorded while the band were "all cabbaged beyond belief".

V – V FESTIVAL 2009, Oasis' last ever gig, or so we thought ...

W – WIBBLING RIVALRY, when interviewer John Harris sat down to interview the brothers, little did he know he was going to record the epic 14 minute, expletive-filled argument that would go on to be released as a bootleg single. Go have a listen (it's not for sensitive ears though!)

X – X (formerly known as Twitter), the social media platform Liam favours for all his infamous sweary rants.

Y – YOGA, Liam once had a mishap on the mat, "I done yoga once and I got stuck".

Z – ZOO, (Hertfordshire Zoo to be exact). Keepers named two endangered African penguin chicks Liam and Noel, dubbed 'little terrors'.

ALL AROUND THE WORLD

Were you one of the lucky few who bagged a ticket? Or have you not stopped crying your heart out since you were kicked out of the ticket queue? The eagerly awaited Live 25 tour kicked off in Cardiff's Principality Stadium in July and eighteen cities later will finish in São Paolo's Estadio MorumBIS in November. Let's take a look at all the stops along the way ...

Time since Oasis gig:

15 YEARS, 10 MONTHS, 12 DAYS

Most popular song:

WONDERWALL

6 Toronto
Rogers Stadium
Capacity: 50,000
24-25 August

9 Los Angeles
Rose Bowl Stadium
Capacity: 90,000
6-7 September

7 Chicago
Soldier Field
Capacity 61,000
28 August

10 Mexico City
Estadio GNP Seguros
Capacity: 65,000
12-13 September

8 East Rutherford
MetLife Stadium
Capacity 82,000
31 August
1 September

17 Santiago
Estadio Nacional
Capacity: 48,000
19 November

18 São Paolo
Estadio MorumBIS
Capacity: 66,000
22-23 November

Total shows: 41

16 Buenos Aires
Estadio River Plate
Capacity: 84,000
15-16 November

CONFIRMED SUPPORT ACTS:
Richard Ashcroft, Cast

64

100% UNOFFICIAL

5 Dublin
Croke Park
Capacity: 82,000
16-17 August

4 Edinburgh
Scottish Gas Murrayfield Stadium
Capacity: 67,000
8-9, 12 August

2 Manchester
Heaton Park
Capacity: 80,000
11-12, 16, 19-20 July

Reported total ticket sales:
£400 MILLION

12 Seoul
Goyang Stadium
Capacity: 41,000
21 October

3 London
Wembley Stadium
Capacity: 90,000
25-26, 30 July
2-3 August

11 London
Wembley Stadium
Capacity: 90,000
27-28 September

13 Tokyo
Tokyo Dome
Capacity: 55,000
25-26 October

1 Cardiff
Principality Stadium
Capacity: 74,000
4-5 July

14 Melbourne
Marvel Stadium
Capacity: 53,000
31 October
1-4 November

LINE UP:
Liam Gallagher
Noel Gallagher
Paul 'Bonehead' Arthurs
Gem Archer
Andy Bell
Zak Starkey

Total countries visited: **11**

Total worldwide audience:
3,150,000

15 Sydney
Accor Stadium
Capacity: 83,000
7-8 November

65

NO CIGARETTES AND ALCOHOL

Liam spent 2025 getting fit for the big gigs and promised to have a booze-free summer so he could "get in the zone of zones", as he said on X.

FREE PETE?
The Libertines' Pete Doherty offered to do a quick acoustic set in return for tickets for his friends and family. Meanwhile, support acts were confirmed as Cast and Richard Ashcroft.

Richard Ashcroft: long-time friend of the band and above Pete Doherty on the support wishlist.

THAT LEAKED SETLIST
When a supposed setlist was shared on X, Liam replied: "It's not far off". He could be messing with fans, or giving a major hint. But what was on it? And where the heck is 'Wonderwall'? Well it's perfect as an encore …

'Acquiesce'
'Some Might Say'
'Lyla'
'Shakermaker'
'The Hindu Times'
'Columbia'
'Cast No Shadow'
'She's Electric'
'Stand By Me'
'Stop Crying Your Heart Out'
'The Importance of Being Idle'
'Half the World Away'
'Whatever'
'Slide Away'
'Supersonic'
'Morning Glory'
'Rock 'n' Roll Star'
'Cigarettes & Alcohol'
'Don't Look Back in Anger'
'Live Forever'
'Champagne Supernova'

Cast: the Liverpudlian legends have the chops (and mops) needed to support Oasis.

KNEBWORTH: THE RETURN?
Oasis shut down rumours they'd play a giant gig at Knebworth in 2026. But, they also said a reunion would never happen, so watch this space …

THE TAYLOR SWIFT EFFECT
When Taylor's Eras tour hit the UK and Ireland, it boosted the economy by nearly £1 billion and it's hoped that the Oasis reunion tour will do the same. It's not just the ticket prices that will encourage fans to splash the cash, but food, travel, hotels and new bucket hats all round.

Get ready for the inevitable surge in bucket hat sales to boost the economy.

Liam: "Are you ready for the encore, Our Kid?"

CREDITS

Front Cover: PICTURES: Alamy Images
2-3: PICTURES: Alamy Images, Shutterstock
4-5: PICTURES: Alamy Images
6-7: PICTURES: Alamy Images, Shutterstock
8-9: PICTURES: Alamy Images
10-11: WORDS: Sunday World, The Big Issue, Radio X
PICTURES: Alamy Images, Shutterstock, YouTube, Liam Gallagher - The River (Official Knebworth 22 Clip)
12-13: PICTURES: Alamy Images, Shutterstock, YouTube, Oasis - Some Might Say (Official HD Remastered Video), Oasis - Roll With It (Official HD Remastered Video), Blur - Country House (Official Music Video), Oasis - Wonderwall (Official HD Remastered Video), Oasis - I Am The Walrus (Live at Knebworth, 11 August '96), Oasis - D'You Know What I Mean? (Official HD Remastered Video), All4, Best of the Word
14-15: PICTURES: Alamy Images, Shutterstock, YouTube, Oasis - Go Let It Out (Official Video), YouTube, Oasis - The Hindu Times (Official Video), Oasis - The Importance Of Being Idle, Oasis - The Shock Of The Lightning (Official Video), Oasis: Supersonic | Official Trailer YouTube
16-17: PICTURES: Alamy Images, Shutterstock
18-19: WORDS: Herald Scotland, Radio X, The Sun
PICTURES: Alamy Images, Shutterstock
20-21: WORDS: Louder Than Sound, BBC News, Buzzfeed
PICTURES: Alamy Images, Shutterstock
22-23: PICTURES: Alamy Images
24-25: PICTURES: Alamy Images
26-27: PICTURES: Alamy Images
28-29: WORDS: Shortlist, YouTube interview, Rolling Stone
PICTURES: Alamy Images, Shutterstock
30-31: WORDS: GQ, GQ US, NME, The Guardian, Blur film: No Distance Left To Run
PICTURES: Alamy Images, Shutterstock
32-33: WORDS: Manchester Evening News
PICTURES: Alamy Images
34-35: WORDS: NME, YouTube interview
PICTURES: Alamy Images, Shutterstock
36-37: PICTURES: Shutterstock, Oasis - All Around The World (Official Video) YouTube, Oasis - Songbird Official Video, YouTube, Oasis - Lyla Official Video YouTube, Oasis - Lord Don't Slow Me Down Official Video, YouTube
38-39: PICTURES: Alamy Images, Shutterstock
40-41: PICTURES: Alamy Images
42-43: WORDS: Heathen Chemistry EPK
PICTURES: Alamy Images, Shutterstock
44-45: WORDS: Spin
PICTURES: Alamy Images, Shutterstock
46-47: PICTURES: Alamy Images, Shutterstock
48-49: WORDS: YouTube interview, Radio X
PICTURES: Alamy Images, Shutterstock
50-51: PICTURES: Alamy Images
52-53: WORDS: Glamour, NME, BBC, Louder
PICTURES: Alamy Images, Shutterstock
54-55: PICTURES: Shutterstock
56-57: WORDS: oasisinet.com
PICTURES: Shutterstock
58: PICTURES: Shutterstock
60-61: PICTURES: Shutterstock
62-63: WORDS: NME, Far Out, The Independent, BBC News, Lad Bible
PICTURES: Alamy Images, Shutterstock, YouTube, Oasis - Acquiesce (Live at Knebworth, 10 August '96)
64-65: Words: NME
66-67: PICTURES: Alamy Images, Shutterstock
70-71: PICTURES: Alamy Images, Shutterstock

ANSWERS

Page 54

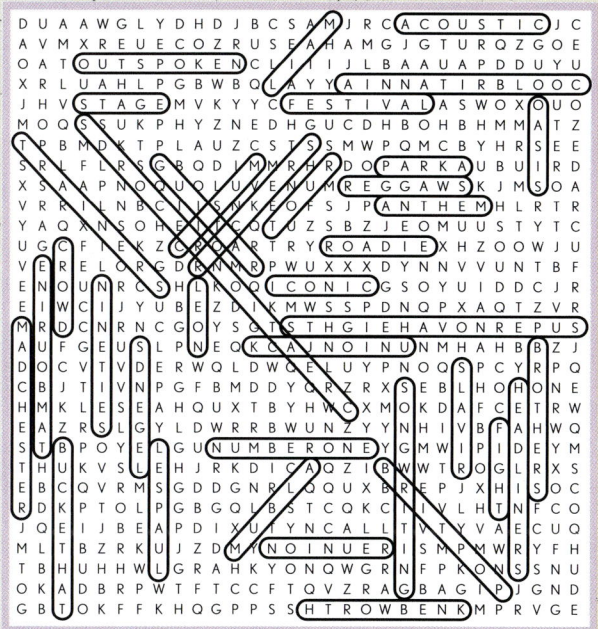

Page 55

CANDID HERMIT WHIRLER
MARRIED WITH CHILDREN

LONGING MORRY
MORNING GLORY

HAKES REMARK
SHAKERMAKER

LOTTI WHIRL
ROLL WITH IT

DAISY WALE
SLIDE AWAY

NERD WALLOW
WONDERWALL

FIRE REVOLVE
LIVE FOREVER

A COWHAND TOSS
CAST NO SHADOW

BIND GROWN INTO
BRING IT ON DOWN

CAVEMAN HANGUP POSER
CHAMPAGNE SUPERNOVA

Page 59

Page 58

1. King Tut's Wah Wah Hut, Glasgow **(1993)**
2. Cliffs Pavilion, Southend **(1995)**
3. Maine Road, Manchester **(March 1996)**
4. Knebworth **(April 1996)**
5. Tour of Brotherly Love **(2000)**
6. Madison Square Garden **(2005)**
7. Rock En Seine **(2009)**
8. Cardiff Principality Stadium **(2025)**

Pages 56-57

1 = J
2 = H
3 = F
4 = D
5 = K
6 = C
7 = I
8 = B
9 = E
10 = A
11 = G

Pages 60-61

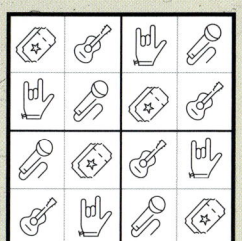
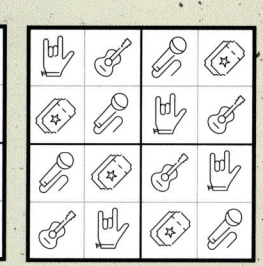
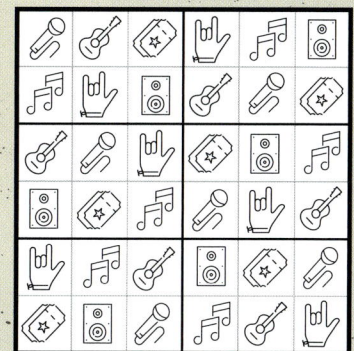
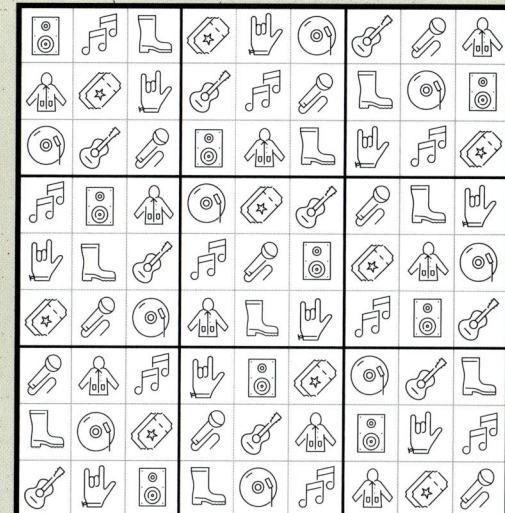